A Supported Employment Workbook

A Supported Employment Workbook

Using Individual Profiling and Job Matching

Steve Leach

Forewords by Stephen Beyer and Dave Willingham

Jessica Kingsley Publishers
London and Philadelphia

First published in the United Kingdom in 2002
by Jessica Kingsley Publishers
116 Pentonville Road
London N1 9JB, UK
and
400 Market Street, Suite 400
Philadelphia, PA 19106, USA

www.jkp.com

Library of Congress Cataloging in Publication Data
A CIP catalog record for this book is available from the Library of Congress

British Library Cataloguing in Publication Data
A CIP catalogue record for this book is available from the British Library

ISBN 978 1 84310 052 2

To Samara, my special daughter,
who always manages to bring me
back to the real world,
sometimes with a hard landing,
but is the one person to
keep me moving forward.
She is cherished beyond measure.

Table of Contents

Foreword

Supported employment is not a fad. It is a concrete set of well researched methods, the worth of which has been recognised and formally pursued as an act of government policy for many years in the USA and Australia and more recently in Norway, Eire, and other European countries.

It has been tried and tested in many other countries, including the UK, through a host of European Union or locally funded development projects. The trend in developed countries has been to have inclusion in the world of employment as part of a civil rights agenda, pursued through the development of more person-centred services.

Supported employment is completely consistent with this trend and where investment has been made in supported employment, it has played a major role in moving the inclusion agenda forward.

Supported employment has not only been good for disabled people; it has also benefited employers. The world of work is changing. The most successful firms are recognising that their workforce is diverse in many ways and that they have to take a positive approach to accommodating that diversity if they are ultimately to be productive and profitable. Disability is only one aspect of diversity. We can become more responsive to diversity, and gain maximum benefit for disabled workers and employers, if we adopt approaches that recognise that people and workplaces are unique and that careful analysis of both person and workplace is needed if a productive and satisfying match is to be produced. Supported employment is just such an approach.

Here in the UK we have invested in government employment services over many years, and have put significant resources into an infrastructure dedicated to the task of finding disabled people employment. Doubts have grown over time about the efficiency of this system and the supported employment critique has played a part in this examination. In addition, we have a large network of employment projects funded by local government, the NHS and the European Union. These are also facing change with new attempts being made to co-ordinate all employment efforts through Welfare to Work Joint Investment Plans. It is a great irony that those who have invested a great deal in a system then have the greatest task in modernising it when change is called for.

There is a great deal of reform underway in the UK, and employment service providers and government face major challenges in managing change in the system, and in learning how supported employment can play a part in the UK reform effort. Staff working in UK employment services are on the front line of this reform. We must not underestimate how difficult they may find changing their practice. They will need investment in training, and information on the most effective ways of working, if they are to make the transition to more person-centred services.

The work presented here provides practical materials to help anyone involved in employment placement to ask the right questions and collect the right information to get to that al- important 'ideal job match'. It is a timely and significant contribution to the individualisation of our employment services.

Dr Stephen Beyer, July 2001
Deputy Director
Welsh Centre for Learning Disabilities
University of Wales College of Medicine

Foreword

Having worked in supported employment for a number of years I have witnessed the success of the philosophies, values and methods discussed in this book for people with learning disabilities, mental health problems and dual diagnosis.

As supported employment has developed and grown, so has the number of definitions, variations and practices. This book draws together the best and most successful elements of these, and emphasises the underlying principles of an individual person-centred approach to supported employment.

The author takes this approach and successfully merges it with a step-by-step guide to working with individuals who have, traditionally, been excluded from the labour market.

The process begins with vocational profiling, an excellent tool for job matching which, in my opinion, should be introduced as standard practice for all agencies. The book then continues right through the training and maintaining elements of supported employment. In a statistics-driven industry, maintaining employment is often secondary to finding jobs.

Maintaining employment is a vital area to consider if we are to stop the cycle of unemployment amongst many disadvantaged groups. This book emphasises the importance of evaluating all aspects of the potential workplace as well as tasks involved, thus reinforcing the job-matching process and increasing the chances of success.

If central government's 'inclusion' agenda is to be made a reality and finances continually squeezed, then the use of natural supports, highlighted in this book, will be increasingly important and this book offers practical and sensible advice to workers supporting individuals in the workplace.

Finally, this book should also be a helpful and interesting workbook for all agencies such as social services and health services, and voluntary and private sectors who may work with supported employment agencies, and should be made available to all 'job developers', whatever their service background.

In short, the UK has long been awaiting a book such as this, and for a practitioner committed to good supported employment practice, it provides an excellent guide to sound practice.

Dave Willingham, July 2001
Supported Employment Co-ordinator
Hartlepool Borough Council

Acknowledgements

It is a pleasure to acknowledge all the work of other practitioners and authors who have helped in the formulation of my thinking in this workbook. Denise Bissonnette, Michael Callahan, Dale DiLeo, David Johnstone, John O'Brien, Michael Oliver, Rachel Perkins, Tony Phillips, Pat Rogan, Tom Shakespeare, Paul Wehman to name but a few. They are too numerous to mention but they help make up a cornerstone of the wider disability and supported employment movement both here and in the USA.

My special thanks to Steve Beyer for his clarity of thought and for his perceptive way of keeping me focused. This support has been vital in the development of a workbook that I hope can be useful in any job development situation for anyone with disabilities who has to overcome barriers to achieving sustainable employment.

To Dave Willingham, Pat Baldwin and Anne O'Bryan for their contributions and enthusiastic encouragement.

To Scope, for continuing to develop its employment services in line with the principles of inclusion and self-determination that form the core of its mission.

To Ken Hawkins for his responsive and considered support.

Risk assessment information reproduced with thanks to Peter Ray.

With grateful thanks to Phil Edwards for his original idea for the matching grid.

Introduction

Working in the field of supported employment in the UK currently is an exciting, challenging and frightening experience. Major changes are being driven by a number of forces. One of these, the disability rights movement, has been asking for evidence of our ability to provide real jobs in real working environments for all people with disabilities. The traditional perspective based on individual limitations is being increasingly challenged and people expect the full range of opportunities, experiences, supports, guarantees and individual rights. There is now the recognition of the rights of people with disabilities, in particular learning difficulties, to:

> ...an ordinary life-style in the community and the chance to pursue socially valued options such as education and work [which] has caused service planners to rethink their provision. (Sutcliffe 1991, p.7)

Another force driving change is the government, whose policy is gradually shifting to encompass legislation that encourages a vision of equality and social inclusion for all within our community; the Disability Discrimination Act (1995) is an example. This trend can be seen particularly in the employment field, as the government seeks to involve people with disabilities and related organisations in the search for inclusive and effective delivery of its services. Examples of this are the New Deal initiative, specifically aimed at improving employment opportunities for young people with disabilities, and the thorough evaluation of the Supported Employment Programme (SEP) that is being carried out including the consultation process and the SEDI projects (Beyer 1998; Employment Service 1999; Yates 1998).

The concept of social inclusion seeks to help people with disabilities overcome the barriers they face as they seek to achieve equality in our society. Among the most daunting are discrimination, fear, ignorance, prejudice and lack of access and equal rights to work opportunities and services. The concept should be seen as the full and equitable involvement of people with disabilities, with all their differences from the 'norm', in all aspects of mainstream society, as a right not a privilege (Johnstone 1998). Important elements of this concept are the individual's right to self-determination, access and equal opportunity. Dignity and self-determination are universal values and should apply universally – to all disadvantaged groups, including people with disabilities.

> More than ever before, disability policy making in Britain has begun to take on the language of rights and participation, as developed within the disabled people's movement. It may not be much, but it is a start. (Priestley 2000, p.435)

The changes that have been universally welcomed have been the affirmation of the need for client-centred planning and the use of the principles of inclusion and self-determination as the foundation for the development of supported employment services.

The supported employment model takes on board this wider vision in order to develop effective supports for people with disabilities that help them achieve sustainable employment opportunities.

- It develops processes that acknowledge employment as a desirable goal for people with disabilities just as it is for all our society.

- It seeks to identify the most 'natural' ways in which we can support people with disabilities in work.

- It recognises that work plays a pivotal role in defining an individual's quality of life and should be seen as an integral part of a person's overall life experience (Callahan and Garner 1997; Wehman and Kregel 1998).

If we believe in these values, then our employment-related planning objectives need to go much further than just job placement, to examine the many ways lives can be enriched, varied and empowered.

The growing knowledge of supported employment amongst individuals and services has led to an upsurge of interest in it, and, as it is based on the same principles being advocated for society as whole, its influence is growing rapidly. This in turn has led to wide-ranging perspectives on supported employment being espoused. It is only right therefore that readers of this book should be offered an explanation of its underpinning values.

The role of the supported employment service and job developers is to:

> …arrange supports for the individual with disabilities in such a way as to promote a long-term employment experience without the need for continued outside support and intervention from a human service source. (Callahan and Garner 1997, p.70)

All supported employment services will need to drive forward the changes that will lead to increased effectiveness. They should be fully committed to developing quality standards and professional services for people with disabilities that are based on the principles of supported employment.

Supported Employment Principles

- Self-determination – to be proactive in making choices about all aspects of your life, even the choices that lead to miscues and have to be re-negotiated.

- Person-centred planning (PCP) – a process of discovery of individual aims, aspirations and skills that focuses on the individual rather than service provision constraints, a collaborative effort by the individual and those willing to commit time and energy to support the individual in achieving his or her goals.

- Social and economic inclusion – regular life experiences that include family, friends, acquaintances, a job and a social life.

- Choice and independence – having the support, advice and information to make real choices and the support to be able to follow through and make those choices a reality.

- No-one is unemployable – all individuals who want to work can work in a job that matches their skills and needs.

- Learn about work in work – people learn about life by living, not by having life experience in segregated life centres. Everyone learns about work in work, making mistakes, making friends and developing skills in real work situations.

Unless your service is based on these fundamental principles, and you achieve the aim of finding open and sustained employment for people with disabilities, then your continued presence in the employment field will be increasingly challenged – a situation that organisations with sheltered workshop provision are finding themselves in at present.

Supported employment services will therefore need to provide a professional service that is open to examination, takes a long-term view and has clear development plans for both employee and employer. We must be accountable to our clients. We need to acknowledge that individuals with disabilities know what is best for them and the support strategy needs to reflect their input, aspirations and dreams.

Given the opportunity to make real, informed choices, people with disabilities want real jobs in real communities. They believe that:

- it is their right to have real jobs for real wages

- sheltered employment is exploitative

- anyone who wants to can work (Wehman and Kregel 1998).

All supported employment services should focus on these two ideas: individual choice and accurate information on jobs and support options. These give individuals the power to make decisions as well as the responsibility to try to accomplish their goals.

We do not have to conform to a rigid formula of job development. All supported employment services will need to gear themselves up for local and individual differences and provide a personal approach.

This book is not only a workbook offering practical advice in the search for long-term, sustainable employment opportunities. It is also a clarion call to all those in the field of supported employment who have seen enough exclusion of people with disabilities from full economic and social participation – for example:

- people with disabilities having 'jobs' that make up a few hours a week and only receiving therapeutic earnings or £15 income disregard

- sheltered workshops worried about their future existence yet not fully responding to the need for the economic and social inclusion and self-determination of the individuals they employ

- local authority day services setting up 'supported employment services' that are based in day centre facilities and seen as part of the daily activities rota

- jobs that only exist because of wage subsidies for employers.

My intention, in writing the book, is to offer suggestions and examples of how those working in this field can become innovative and proactive facilitators using a variety of techniques, and have the principles of inclusion and self-determination at heart, thus leading to successful, sustainable and long-term employment. Let's be clear about one thing, this is not a complex strategy. But it is time consuming, because it is necessary to be thorough and to focus on the development of opportunities for each person.

Supported employment is a process that is part of a whole life strategy, helping people become fully included in society both economically and socially. It is not forcing people into a job because it is available and makes the state financially better off. Supported employment gives back control to individuals who, with the help of professionals and services working to 'upset' the status quo, will try to achieve their dreams and aspirations for a better life.

This is not to suggest that in the grand scheme of things our efforts are anything other than fairly insignificant, but with commitment, belief and a willingness to create solutions we can make a difference for someone. Be confident:

> ...it's not what we are that holds us back, but what we think we aren't! (Bissonnette 1994, p.16).

The approach adopted in this book covers the whole supported employment process and, whilst it may appear to be focused on a methodical and formal paper-based approach, it is proving to be successful in helping people with disabilities into real, sustainable employment. For example, the Supported Employment Development Initiative (SEDI) projects, funded via The Employment Service, are using similar approaches and having some considerable success.

This approach also tries to be transparent and, therefore, is accountable to all parties. Persevere with a clear commitment to the principles of supported employment and you should be well on the way to providing a successful and inclusive service.

Before examining the individual profiling and job-matching process, a number of topical issues currently being aired in the supported employment field will be considered, as they will have major repercussions on its future development.

Quality standards and professionalisation

Organisations will face many challenges in developing a supported employment service, not least of which will be the need to ensure that the service is inclusive, advocates self-determination and is based on person-centred planning (PCP). Quality standards based on these principles, organisational efficiency and delivering an effective service to individuals will be pre-requisites for all service providers if they wish to have a long-term future in this field.

Not only will the funding agency need to be convinced that the service provided is efficient in terms of the targets set, but individuals and their representatives will also need to be convinced that the service is effective in providing real opportunities to enable them to attain long-term, sustainable jobs based on their choices, needs and aspirations.

Employers will also need to be convinced that the service is providing them with the necessary support to fulfil the job requirements as well as developing an employee who will be a long-term asset to the company. Providers' effectiveness should not just be measured by the number of staff attaining national occupational standards but by their ability to use the principles and practices of supported employment to achieve individual goals.

The government have identified some standards seen to relate to the disability field; recruitment consultancy, advice and guidance, counselling, youth and community work and coaching and mentoring. The professional and higher education qualifications identified are Careers Guidance, Youth Work, Community Work, Social Service and Specialist Disability Provision. The omission of supported employment from this list, if not rectified, will be a major concern for the future of developing a national strategy for effective supported employment services.

Training is important, and active learning on courses such as the Diploma in Supported Employment and the Certificate in Supported Employment is the most useful for work in this field, as the courses give participants a grounding in the principles and practices of SE. An understanding of these principles, ongoing evaluation of service delivery based on quality standards and an innovative and dynamic approach to job development should be the basis for service development.

The exclusion of small, independently funded supported employment agencies and local authority services from the central government funding for supported employment needs to be addressed. If some smaller agencies are achieving the aims of the quality standards but have no staff qualified in the new occupational standards then this should not stop funding moving quickly from the ineffective services to those agencies that are actually delivering real jobs.

The move to ensuring that the minimum support necessary is offered to achieve the client's goals means that natural supports are used in preference to outside job supporters. Does this mean that co-workers will have to train in the new occupational standards as well? If the job supporter, employed by the employer, needs to be certificated, we may find that very few supporters come forward.

If the quality standards are to be effective, they need to be based on the principles of supported employment and not just on targets that only achieve a minimum compliance without achieving individual goals.

Professional qualifications and training will be positive additions to the tools a service has to achieve its aims. However, they need to be based on the principles and practice of supported employment. The Certificate and the Diploma in Supported Employment are the most effective training programmes that, coupled with a comprehensive ongoing evaluation strategy, will lead to long-term improvement.

What would be wholly regressive in the continuing development of effective supported employment services would be an announcement by authorities that 'supported employment services should only be provided by qualified professionals'. We should face directly the issue of national occupational standards and find a way in which quality standards and a professional approach can be nationally developed without stifling the truly innovative and client-centred approaches of supported employment services.

Wage subsidy and inclusion

It is also appropriate to tackle the thorny issue of wage subsidy here and try to end the argument that small supported employment agencies offering job coaches are the only providers of supported employment and SEP contractors only offer the discredited wage subsidy to 'bribe' employers into offering people with disabilities sub-standard employment.

Whilst there are dedicated, principled and effective supported employment agencies out there, can or should offering people with disabilities work experience using therapeutic earnings long term (over six months) or wage disregard using external job coaches to complete the job tasks, with little or no chance of development into sustainable employment, be called supported employment? It is, in effect, an off-site day-service provision that will not lead to independence or self-determination. You may have the most positive client-centred approach in the country, but if you do not get real jobs at real rates of pay, you are not providing an effective, inclusive supported employment service. A recent study in Liverpool concluded:

> Whilst supported employment has demonstrated the capacity to obtain real jobs for people with severe difficulties, they tend to work fewer hours, to be unpaid and be less well integrated. The greatest area of concern is financial: some people are doing productive work, yet are financially worse off for going to work. Supported employment agencies, purchasers, care managers, and users should be aware of the high standards that supported employment is capable of delivering, and not accept second best. (Bass 2000)

This situation may well suit some people and they make a positive decision to continue with it based on their particular circumstances. However, it is usually forced upon people because of the financial constraints and punitive regulations imposed by the benefits system and it rarely, if ever, leads to unsupported employment and independent living.

On the other hand, sustaining employment for people with disabilities only by use of a wage subsidy to an employer, linked to the percentage of non-productivity of the client, even if the client is paid the rate for the job, is also not supported employment, as it is not inclusive and also rarely leads to unsupported employment. You may have each client on a full wage but if he or she is legally employed by the contractor, tied to the employer by subsidy and unable to determine his or her own future, then you are not providing an effective, inclusive supported employment service.

The answer to achieving a quality supported employment service must lie somewhere in between by taking the best of both systems and changing them into one that offers the best possible opportunity for the client to achieve sustainable, long-term employment.

This is not to say that some people will never need long-term support delivered by an effective supported employment service, but it is acknowledging that support must:

- be the minimum required

- be relevant to the particular situation

- have individual development as a primary goal

- have ongoing reviews

- be seen as a natural process.

Any supported employment service needs to be based on clear principles of inclusion and self-determinism and offer a professional service:

- There needs to be a client-centred approach to individual profiling and job matching.

- Development of a positive relationship between the client and the employer is vital.

- All clients must be legally employed by the company not the supported employment contractor.

- We need to identify and use natural, in-house supports whenever possible – this may mean funding the employer specifically for this service.

- We need to ensure that training is offered – this may mean funding internal or external training.

- We need formal, agreed development plans in place, subject to ongoing review.

- We need to ensure that fading support, including job supporters, funding and differences, is the norm and that the development plans ensure that there is commitment to progression.

- We need to fully support the client's development – this could mean challenging the employer's misperceptions or prejudices in a forthright way.

- We need to ensure that employees are aware of their rights and their responsibilities.

- We need to allow people the opportunity to make choices – even if, in our eyes, they are the wrong ones. We offer support and advice but not in the day service tradition of 'care and control'. We all have enough difficulties controlling our own lives without taking on the responsibility for controlling the lives of others.

- We offer an employment service – we are not in loco parentis.

Providing the minimum support necessary to achieve progression and a real job in a real working environment can work for anyone. The more natural that support the more included the individual will be and the more effective the development of a positive relationship between the individual and the employer; the better the chance of gaining long-term, sustainable unsupported employment.

If funding a co-worker, via the employer, to support the individual is the most effective and natural method of developing the individual's skills, then so be it. Job coaching can be useful but is always second best. Identify an appropriate co-worker, making sure he or she understands the individual's needs and, in many cases, a natural learning relationship will develop with little need for outside interference.

Stress and employment development

There is a genuine concern on the part of disabled workers and people working in supported employment about what progression will mean. Will people be left to struggle by themselves in a hostile working environment? This fear and uncertainty is leading both individuals and organisations to criticise supported employment.

There is an argument that it is inappropriate for some people with disabilities, particularly with deteriorating conditions or severe mental, physical and learning disabilities, to pursue this job development approach, using the vocational profile and job analysis. The argument goes that these individuals won't develop, would get too stressed at the thought of progression and just need a little job with an employer who is happy to continue getting a wage subsidy, or that they should continue on therapeutic earnings or seek the security of a segregated workshop.

This is doing those clients a disservice and creating an attitude of charitable donation amongst employers and leading to service control over the choices an individual makes. We need to ensure that the support we offer is appropriate and subject to ongoing review. We need to identify any changes needed, any progression or achievements. Everyone deserves to have his or her skills and successes recognised. We have a responsibility to the individual client and to people with disabilities as a group to enable them to reach their developmental potential.

The argument that it causes too much stress is also a smoke screen for continued inactivity. Employment is a stressful aspect of life for all people and there is no evidence that it is more stressful to people with disabilities or mental health problems than for anyone else. In fact, there is evidence to the contrary (Kroese, Kahn and Hearn 1996). It is how we help the client deal with work stress that is the key to development. Everyone has both rights and responsibilities in the work situation and we have to encourage individuals when making choices to consider all aspects of the job.

Supported employment services offer a service that has at its heart the idea that with support anyone who wants to work can work. It is no longer acceptable for us to be offering that support to clients who are capable of working successfully in open employment or with a reduced amount of support. Such a course of action will only have a detrimental effect on the many others who need that support. We need to ensure that each person is supported to develop to their full potential and this can mean 'stretching' them to attain that potential.

What we should be highlighting are the real successes of supported employment in helping people with disabilities achieve long-term and sustainable employment in areas that use their skills for wages that are the same as for others working in the same jobs. Supported employment aims to provide the minimum support necessary for each person to achieve as much as he or she can, whether this is in unsupported employment or with continuing support in whatever form is appropriate.

The justification of seeing supported employment in terms of development for all and progression to unsupported employment where possible is to ensure that all people are supported effectively and efficiently and no-one is left in a job just because it is a job. With a new emphasis on bringing together all approaches to support – natural supports, job coaches, accommodations, funding and job matching – we are trying to bring an expectation of success and development rather than stagnation and control.

Who is the book for?

The fundamental change in the relationship between individual and service agency or professional means that the traditional methods of evaluating eligibility or employment 'potential' will also have to change.

This book offers advice and examples of how to develop a strategy to ensure that your service provision is based on the principles of supported employment and uses a methodology for providing effective and efficient support to both employee and employer in their quest for a successful job match.

The book's primary target audience is all job developers working in the supported employment field: SEP/Workstep contractors, supported employment agencies, local authorities with supported employment provision and sheltered workshops, Disability Employment Advisers (DEAs), other employment service advisers, community mental health teams, college tutors supporting young people with disabilities. In fact, all those trying to move their service forward into progressing people into open employment and into all aspects of our society. It would also be a useful study book for those involved in undertaking any courses or training in supported employment, offering a set of materials that covers all aspects of the process.

All agencies, both independent and allied to social services, health trusts and local authorities should find it helpful to examine their current practice in finding real paid jobs for all clients. If your service, whatever its background or provision base, works positively and effectively for the most appropriate and sustainable outcome in a client-centred way, then the strategy advocated in this book will be a positive addition to the tools you use. It won't work in every case and when it doesn't – learn and move on.

This book is not a rigid set of rules but a flexible guide to the principles underpinning the service and ways in which a support strategy using those principles can be developed in partnership with both the employee and employer.

Any supported employment service – supporting individuals inclusively and effectively and evaluating and managing that service – is going to have to be open to quality review. It is therefore imperative that we develop a process that is capable of fulfilling the needs of our customers and is one that:

- is based on the principles of supported employment

- has a client-centred approach

- promotes service accountability

- works to agreed quality standards

- achieves progression through sustainable employment.

This means ensuring that your service approach is both open and transparent. If you are to provide a quality service you will need to ensure that your systems for delivering that service are all in place; the forms are completed by setting agreed objectives and shared with the client, schedules kept, appropriate support offered, negotiations undertaken, monitoring is effective and an evaluation strategy for all these elements is agreed. The main aim of the service is not only to raise self-esteem. It is to ensure that the individuals, through determining their own aims and aspirations, achieve sustainable, paid open employment and that you offer the choices that can accomplish those goals.

This book is a practical tool for all job developers and offers ideas based on real situations. There will also be a number of practical exercises throughout to help you get to grip with the ideas and materials.

I should also make it clear that the term 'job developer' is not a professional term for all qualified and trained staff; it is a general term for anyone involved in finding jobs for people with disabilities. Parents, carers, family and friends are all important 'job developers' and it is essential that they support the people they care for in a way that develops independence. I believe that they have as much to gain from this workbook as the professionals working in the field.

This book draws on the extensive work carried out in the USA, the Policy Consortium Group as detailed in a recent publication *Supported Employment: A National Framework* (O'Bryan *et al.* 2000) and the Supported Employment Development Initiative (SEDI) project 'Scope To Work', which the author is coordinating nationally for Scope.

It is a simple but resource-hungry process, and it is not a plan that will guarantee success; it is a strategy that will ensure that you offer the best opportunity possible for individuals to get a job doing things that they are interested in and that the employer accepts is supporting their business to move forward.

The process will and should raise more questions than it answers but this is as it should be – a flexible, dynamic process will need solutions found along the way and predetermined actions relating to expected outcomes would not be helpful.

Chapter 1

The Supported Employment Process

Supported employment focuses on work, not getting ready for work, not on having all of the skills before going to work, and not on meeting human services criteria before entering the competitive job market. The individual must simply want to work... (Wehman and Kregel 1998, p.153)

Definition of supported employment

For the purpose of clarity, the following definition of supported employment will be used as the foundation for the support process described in the workbook.

> Supported employment is a way of enabling people who need additional support to succeed in real, long-term and sustainable employment.

Aims of supported employment

The following aims follow on from this definition and the support process.

- People are hired and paid by an employer.
- They receive full employee entitlements.
- The job meets the employee's aspirations for work.

- The work meets the employer's requirements.

- The employee and employer receive the minimum support necessary to ensure success.

Flexibility v. rigidity

One final note of caution before we discuss the strategy in depth. The forms included in this book are there as a guide for you and the client. Do not follow them inflexibly; use them as tools to tease out the information that helps you and the client make effective job-matching choices. Ensure that all parties agree openly to the plan you advise as being the best course of action. If you don't complete all parts of the forms, ask yourself and the client:

- Do we have a clear picture of the client's needs and aspirations without the missing information?

- Can we make an effective evaluation without the missing information?

- Is it going to be too stressful to the client to gain the missing information?

If your answer to these questions is 'yes', then consider proceeding without the information. If, however, your answer is 'no', then consider how detrimental the lack of information is:

- Does it indicate a lack of commitment on the part of the client?

- Will a development plan be compromised without it?

- Does the client understand the pitfalls of not supplying the information?

Do not let the forms get in the way of the natural process that matches client to job. Use the person you are supporting to clarify any confusions or gaps, make sure he or she is fully involved in the process and really makes the decisions rather than trying to please you. Unless the choices made are, in practical terms, impossible to achieve then think positively about what resources you will need to achieve a successful conclusion.

Individual profiling and job-matching process

This model has at its heart the notion that almost anyone can find paid employment if support is provided. The key points to be made that define the stages of the supported employment process are:

1. The client-centred analysis of individual strengths and preferences forms the basis of this strategy, the aim being to find paid employment for people with disabilities in regular work situations, that tries to match their skills, preferences and aspirations. It involves assisting adults with disabilities to take responsibility for their employability, make choices about the work they want and increase the likelihood of job satisfaction and sustainable employment.

2. This should be achieved by assessing those skills and preferences for each individual involved with this initiative – providing appropriate individualised support. This could be in the workplace via a support worker, training opportunities for the employer and/or employee, short-term funding or other support to enable the individual to achieve integration and interaction in the workplace with work colleagues.

3. Employment opportunities for people with disabilities should be the same as for everyone else: real jobs paid at the going rate, with safe working conditions and opportunities for progression. The companies in turn should receive support and expertise to develop the skills to maximise each employee's potential.

4. The client's needs and employer's needs are dynamic and in a permanent state of change; therefore, the focus should be on developing the means by which any 'gaps' can be minimised, with remaining elements accommodated by negotiation. It can also develop strategies for both parties to continue to overcome any mismatches to ensure sustainable employment at an appropriate level.

5. Establishing or improving relationships between employee and employer is an important element in the job-matching process and an opportunity can stand or fall on this alone. Whatever the initial support needs, establishing relationships between employers and jobseekers/ employees is the eventual goal of supported employment agencies and leads to open employment being considered.

6. The most important role of the job developer in the supported employment process is that of a catalyst. This also has direct implications for the level of support offered: there is a need to offer the minimum level of effective support and also to use the in-house support mechanisms wherever possible.

7. Clear, careful planning is needed to avoid 'crisis calls'. The goal to achieve is that of giving the employee the chance of becoming a contributing and valued member of the workforce. The quicker the job developer is able to help build a positive working relationship between the employee, co-workers and employer, the sooner this goal will be achieved. The job developer is on the periphery and should be considered a resource not a dependency.

8. The involvement of co-workers in the task analysis and job-matching process recognises the contribution they can make and paves the way for the establishment of a positive relationship. The job developer needs to ensure that, if necessary, the co-worker is involved when the employee starts work with the support worker advising from the background. If they are involved, co-workers are much more likely to feel welcoming to the new employee. At the same time, they provide valuable information for the job-matching process.

9. A key feature of this strategy, then, is the need to use well trained and experienced job developers with the skills to support the participants, their co-workers and employers responsible for supervising people with severe disabilities in typical jobs and workplaces. The job developer needs to have an overview of this model's aims and objectives and focus on identifying and integrating all available sources of support. Using other agencies with particular skills should also be considered.

10. The client-centred approach coupled with an imaginative use of resources (including energy, time and ideas, not just money) will be used to the best effect in resolving areas of difficulty. It is a model in which an employer is offered a range of support, including, in some appropriate circumstances, financial support on a tapering basis, with a clear goal of open employment. This enables a positive relationship to develop between employee and employer that is going to offer an improved level of progression. There will be a clarity of objective to which all parties agree from the first, thus avoiding the problems that arise when it is felt that the goalposts have been moved.

The process is shown diagrammatically in Figure 1.1 at the end of this chapter. The main elements in the process have been outlined in the box below.

Supported Employment Process

Initial contact (referral process)

Vocational profiling, including job tasters

> Development Plan (part one)

Job search and marketing

> Job finding
>
> Marketing
>
> Potential jobs

Job analysis

> Job matching
>
> Task analysis
>
> Development Plan (part two)

Support review process

> Ongoing Support Review (OSR)
>
> Development Plan (part three)
>
> Support Review Chart (SRC)
>
> Overall Job Review (OJR)
>
> Development Plan (part four)

Progression to unsupported employment

> Post-progression support

For any particular client you may shortcut the strategy for a number of reasons, e.g. a person who self-refers may already have an employer in mind that is willing to support him or her. Job search, therefore, is not necessary at this stage unless the potential job falls through.

It is strongly recommended that whatever the circumstances, the vocational profile and job analysis should be completed, as they are crucial elements to ensure you identify the most appropriate and minimum support necessary to achieve individual goals.

Copy all the materials which are in the Appendices at the back of the book and 'experiment' with family, friends and colleagues to gain an insight into their use in the field. At least read the materials to familiarise yourself with the process.

The overall plan (see Figure 1.1) encompasses all the elements of a new inclusive supported employment service and the sections of this guide relate to each of the process elements. Most of you will be very familiar with most of the elements in one form or another. I am not trying to teach grandmothers the art of egg-sucking, but to put a freshness back into the strategies being used to coincide with the new drive to develop a national framework for supported employment. It is hoped that this workbook will help reinforce existing good practices and offer ideas, examples and references, to help you to continue to develop better ones.

The only unfamiliar element will probably be the Support Review Chart (SRC) that will be discussed fully later in the book. I will say, however, that it has been developed in order to improve the connection between employee and employer.

It is fully acknowledged that there will be some clients who will need long-term supported employment. However, it is right that their support is still developmental in nature, geared towards ensuring that the support is always the minimum necessary for success; whether that is progression to unsupported employment or continued supported employment.

The need is to focus on specific development areas and unresolved issues as well as specific details of client progression. This will help both client and employer formally acknowledge the progression made, offering concrete examples and challenging preconceived notions about a person's skills and development potential. It is a tool to aid the fading process, i.e. the reduction of support as skills increase and the relationship strengthens between employee and employer that leads to unsupported employment.

Whilst the fading process actually starts from day one of the initial negotiation for the job, the hardest part of it is to gain 'closure', the final few steps of the process. The Support Review Chart (Appendix 9) will help in that final stage. From practical experience, employers, when faced with overwhelming evidence of progression (with which they have been involved), will accept the need to move further along the road and deliver what was agreed – a long-term job.

This is not a purely linear progression, as can be seen from the diagram in Figure 1.1, and allows for the return to an earlier part of the process or even referral out of the process. You cannot support everyone so use appropriate alternatives.

As you follow the process in the workbook you will come across case studies and exercises. It is for you to decide whether you complete the exercises or not, but if you want to begin to appraise the usefulness of following all or part of the process I would suggest that you need to see how the process works. Learn and move on.

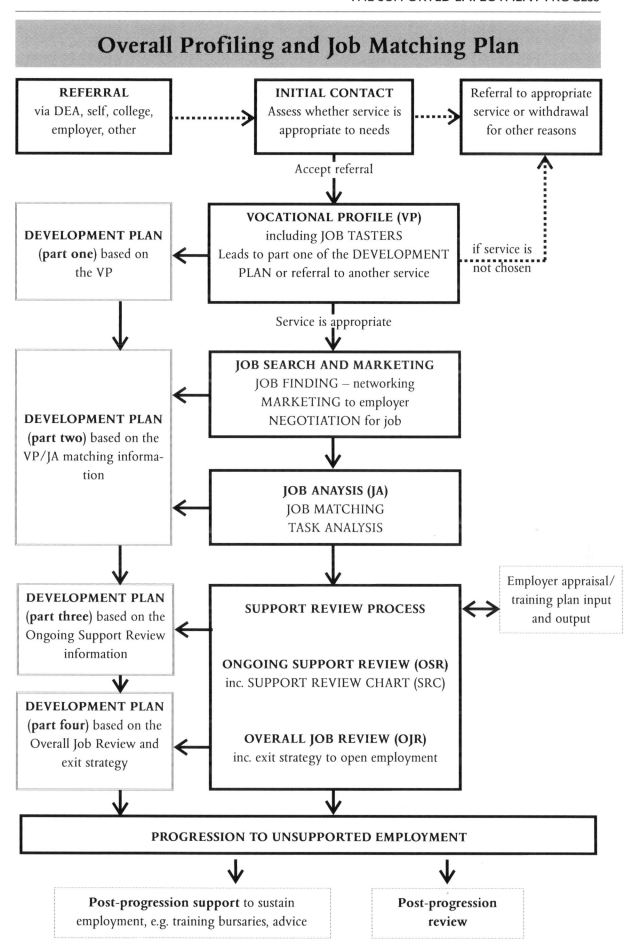

Figure 1.1 Overall Profiling and Job Matching Plan

Chapter 2

Initial Contact

There will always be a broad range of referral agencies: DEAs, colleges, community workers, employers, and self-referrals. It is therefore useful to ensure that you have a way of collating all the initial contact information. An example of an initial contact form is shown in Appendix 1.

This form should show basic personal information of the potential client, referrer and any potential employment opportunity. Some of this information is useful immediately in the job search strategy but some will be useful at a later stage as part of a regular review of the service organisation. It will help assess the quality of your service delivery, the make-up of your client base (e.g. where they come from) and whether there are any improvements you can make in this initial contact procedure. Relevant information will help ensure appropriate support is offered now and in the future.

For Workstep contractors wanting to ensure that any referral not coming via the DEA (we have to assume that DEA referrals will be eligible) is covered by the funding arrangements, approval from the DEA that the person fulfils the Workstep eligibility criteria will have to be obtained prior to starting the profiling process. These criteria will be specified in the new Employment Service regulations, briefly outlined in the box below.

Workstep Eligibility Criteria

All eligible people must be disabled, as defined by the Disability Discrimination Act 1995. This Act defines a disabled person as a person who has 'a physical or mental impairment which has a substantial and long-term adverse effect on his/her ability to carry out normal day-to-day activities'.

In addition, eligible people must also fall within one of the following groups of people who are:

1. On Incapacity Benefits (including Severe Disablement Allowance and Income Support) or

2. On Jobseekers Allowance (JSA), and/or NI credits only, for 6 months or more or

3. On Jobseekers Allowance (JSA), and/or NI credits only, for less than 6 months but have been in receipt of Incapacity Benefit immediately before claiming Jobseekers Allowance or

4. A former supported employee who has progressed but needs to return to the programme within 2 years or has left for other reasons and returns within one year or

5. Currently in work but at serious risk of losing their job as a result of disability, even after the employer has made all reasonable adjustments and considered other available support options or

6. Ineligible to claim Incapacity Benefits as a non-claimant returner to the labour market or a recent/prospective full-time education or training leaver.

(The Employment Service 2001, p.9)

It should be noted, however, that these criteria are already the subject of change, as providers are challenging the validity and clarity of the eligibility criteria that exclude people who would previously have been eligible. Criteron 6, in particular, is under review and will probably be replaced.

Having established contact you will need to have an initial meeting with the individual and discuss the support your service can offer and decide in conjunction with him or her whether the service is appropriate for his or her needs and outline an action plan. See Case Study 2.1.

Case Study 2.1

James, referred by a community outreach worker, felt that the job-matching process was a very good idea as he had only a vague idea about how his skills related to work opportunities. We decided over the phone to plan for our first meeting as follows:

- I would send a vocational profile form for him to complete with the support of his brother (who acts as James' 'writer' for more complex documents).

- He would discuss relevant areas of the profile with his mother and brother, asking them how they consider such areas as motivations, job tasks, likes and dislikes etc. in their present employment.

- He would look at some possible job areas, considering good points and bad points and skills required.

- We arranged to meet in three weeks time at our local office. (He wanted to be there on his own to discuss next steps.)

- We would then consider potential job tasters for him to get a more 'hands on' view of appropriate working environments.

- This would be followed by a review of any future plans for support from our service.

If your service is not appropriate for the client then you will need to refer him or her back to the DEA or to a more appropriate service, e.g. a specialist disability service, college, voluntary services.

If both you and the client decide to continue then you need to arrange a longer meeting either to start the vocational profile or to discuss the profile information that the individual, with or without the help of an advocate, has already collated (if the vocational profile has been sent prior to any meeting).

It is always advisable to try and get the client to consider the profile before the first meeting. This will give the client time to reflect on the information required and he or she may be able to call on the support of a friend or advocate to ensure that as much information as possible is given. To summarise:

- Collate all initial contact information in an easy and simple format.

- Establish whether your service is appropriate.

- Arrange an individual initial meeting to discuss client goals.

- Discuss the vocational profile, job-matching process and service strategy.

- Plan an agreed course of action that will start to achieve the aims and aspirations initially identified by the client.

Now complete Exercise 2.1.

Exercise 2.1

Copy and complete the initial contact form (Appendix 1a) for one of your existing clients.
- Did you have all the necessary information to hand?
- Did you need all the information?
- Do you have other requirements that need to be added to the form?
- Can you see a need for changes in your service procedure?

Chapter 3

The Vocational Profile

Introduction

This chapter looks at elements of the vocational profile and offers advice and examples to help you complete it as fully as possible. See Appendix 2a for a copy of the form.

The main principle of the vocational profiling process is to focus on the individual who is at the centre of your job development strategy. An understanding of the client's whole life spectrum will inform this process. Likes and dislikes, interests, hobbies, motivations, current life plans, are all contributions that will become part of the profiling process, which creatively identifies all the ingredients of a viable job for the client.

Vocational profiling is firmly centred in an approach that balances the assessment of the person with the characteristics of the environment in which they will work in order to achieve a successful job match and, therefore, long-term sustainable employment.

Remember, vocational profiling is a process not a form and the important point is to get to know the client, not make sure every part of the form is completed, regardless of how relevant it is to the particular client. It is also important to consider carefully the location of this first meeting and be guided by the client.

You need to ensure that the client is calm and relaxed if you wish to get an in-depth profile that could include some very personal and sensitive information. Some clients may find the comfort and security of their home the most suitable place for this first meeting; others may want a neutral, quiet place or be happy with your local office. Others may want to meet in a favourite café. If you can accommodate these requests it may result in a much more useful profile. This may be time-consuming but will save time later when the picture you have of the client leads to a well formulated development plan, and you can both focus on jobs that fulfil the client's profile.

Whilst completing the profile, consider the following:

- The information collected during profiling should be derived from natural sources, rather than those set up specifically for the purposes of evaluation – i.e. 'live' information, not formal assessment test data.

- Information obtained through profiling is to be used as a guide to help your service find suitable jobs for people, not to exclude people from particular jobs – e.g. 'J cannot read, therefore he cannot work in an office base'.

- The main purpose of vocational profiling is to collect information about a person rather than use it to assess his or her potential for obtaining employment.

- Information contained in the profile should be based on the individual's whole life, and not just taken from a sample of a person's work performance.

- The information should not be used as the perfect job-matching tool. It is the individual who will ultimately determine the success of the job match. Some successful job opportunities are based on unfavourable job matches in which particular circumstances make it work.

- The individual's perception of his or her situation, skills and preferences is important, but there is other information, from a family member, employer or even you as the job developer, which will help formulate a clearer picture in order for you to offer the most effective support.

- The profile should be should be descriptive and written in full sentences. See Case Study 3.1.

The vocational profile will be a dynamic information base; as the person has wider work experience and training their perception of work and their preferences may well change. This means that the vocational profile has to be regularly reviewed and updated. See Case Studies 3.2 and 3.3.

Case Study 3.1

'James doesn't like being in large crowds' is not enough. Describe the actual situation: 'James was observed to get visibly upset when in the middle of a large crowd at the conference and asked to leave. He said that sometimes it worries him but if given a few minutes on his own or with another person he is then OK.'

This gives both you and James a clear picture of the issues that may need to be faced in an employment situation and doesn't dismiss James from being involved in a whole range of social situations.

Case Study 3.2

John, a 26-year-old with learning difficulties, worked in a factory cleaning up and doing some basic maintenance work. After six months in the job he began to arrive late for work or even not turn up on occasion. He sometimes missed jobs that he had previously completed with no problems. The supervisor was at a loss to explain this and John didn't offer any reasons. Having been called in to support John it was discovered that John had been working with the maintenance engineer for a couple of weeks whilst someone was on sick leave and had enjoyed this work a great deal and been very helpful. When the person returned from sick leave John was sent back to do his regular duties. This is when the problems started. We looked into the work schedules and found that some of these maintenance duties were not being done on a regular basis because of manpower constraints, whilst John was under-utilised in his regular duties. With a little flexibility we found that John could work on his own duties every morning and then help the maintenance engineer in the afternoons. This gave John a great incentive to complete his tasks promptly and effectively and to get to work on time in order to accomplish all his regular duties. It also meant that maintenance tasks could be completed on time. If there had been a regular review of John's profile the initial problems may have been avoided.

Case Study 3.3

Peter, a 31-year-old with cerebral palsy, works in a small office undertaking admin duties for front line staff. In his first vocational profile he expressed a clear preference for 'back-room' work. Whilst his job had been involved in the admin support duties, he had on occasion checked some completed forms with the customers on the front line. Over six months he had begun to enjoy these face-to-face duties quite a lot and at his vocational profile review expressed the wish to increase these front-line duties. It was arranged that following some customer relation and computer-use training he would work two days a week on the front line. He now works full-time on the front line and has progressed to open employment.

It is also important to understand that family and friends are stakeholders in this process and their support and contributions can make the difference between success and failure. They may well have a range of contacts through their own work, friends and other activities that could lead to a positive job contact.

A note of caution, however: be aware of the need for a balance between the personal choice, self-determination and independence of the individual and the involvement of family in the supported employment process. Proceed by agreeing all contacts with the individual first. Consider how a job will affect the current family circumstances – changes in benefits, support system, or transport for instance. You also need to identify the new types of family commitment that might be needed to make the job sustainable – getting to work, other adaptations or other social supports.

Whilst the accuracy of the information in the profile is the key to a successful job match it should be recognised that, as with all requests for personal information, particularly in relation to seeking a job, there may be inconsistencies, omissions or inaccuracies. What is important is the discussion during the reviews, testing the information in real job situations through job tasters, and planning a course of action to achieve the client's goals.

If, for instance, the client has indicated that he or she has no difficulty reading but there is a concern that this might not be accurate then it would be useful to arrange a short job taster to verify this aspect. This may be the source of some stress for both you and the client but it is far better to find out this information now than when a job has been arranged and it fails because there are major mismatches between the individual's skills and the needs of the job.

Conversely, it is not necessary to ensure that all 'gaps' are filled right from the start. No job will be ideal and there will be changes to be sorted out during the course of the job. Remember, the vocational profile is not to be used to exclude a client from a particular job. Even if there are 'gaps' in the available support the client may still choose to accept the job and it will then be your role to support that choice wherever possible.

What is important is that you offer a professional service to both client and employer. You should reduce the known gaps prior to job matching or have an effective programme of support to ensure that both client and employer are confident that you are able to support them effectively and that the relationship developing between client and employer is not damaged by problems that could have been foreseen.

You will not be able to cover all bases, and there will be times when no matter how thorough you have been problems will arise at the last minute or well into the job-matching process. Don't despair! If this happens you will have to try to repair the damage by focusing on the particular issue and putting a strategy into place that will alleviate the problem. This may mean changes for either the client or employer or both, but it will be essential to get agreement from both parties for the plan to work. Learn and move on.

Please use these notes as a guide to support you when undertaking a vocational profile with an employee. They are an aid to help make the process as effective as possible in order that the employee can express his or her preferences, experiences and aspirations clearly and concisely.

The forms are worded as if clients complete them themselves but it may be that they wish to complete them either with the help of an independent advocate or with your help. In either situation it is important to ensure that clients understand and agree with the information that is collected.

Either the client or you may find that some of the elements are not relevant or need rewording – do so – this is not the last word in vocational profiles, it is a thought-provoking exercise.

Now complete Exercise 3.1.

Exercise 3.1

Copy the vocational profile in Appendix 2 and complete for yourself as fully as possible.

Make two copies of the preference grid (Section 6) and, as honestly as possible, complete one for your ideal job and one for your present job.

- How close is your job to your ideal job?
- If it is so, what makes it a close match?
- Are there any mismatches or gaps?
- Is there anything you can do to close those gaps?
- Are there parts of your job that outweigh any other parts and in turn keep you motivated?

Vocational profile sections

We will now consider each section of the profile in more detail. Have a copy of the profile to hand for reference.

Life Experiences (Residential / Community)

It is always helpful and can relax the person completing any form to be able to start out positively and actively. All clients will have something to say about their life experiences and this section may encourage them to express themselves positively and fully, drawing out their hopes, fears and dreams. Let people have their say and note down all details. It can also be useful to get information on the more mundane, everyday aspects of living.

DOMESTIC SKILLS

- How regularly does he/she undertake household chores?
- Which ones are liked/disliked and why?

These are complex skills to undertake and may indicate transferable abilities in complex work-related skills.

USE OF COMMUNITY RESOURCES

- Does the client go to the library, cinema, local shops, advice centres, local authority offices, parks, or museums?

- How regularly and is it on his/her own or with someone?

- What does he/she like/dislike about these excursions?

- Can the client use public transport on his/her own?

- Can the client find his/her way around?

All these skills indicate a level of initiative and responsibility that has implications for the work environment.

COMMUNICATION SKILLS

- Are there any concerns about the client's visual, hearing, listening or speaking skills? Does he/she have any difficulties because of physical conditions or with social situations, e.g. withdrawal when in small/large groups or in one-to-one situations?

- Does the client have any difficulties in understanding what is being said?

- Does he/she prefer certain ways of communicating?

See Case Study 3.4.

Case Study 3.4

Helen, a woman of 30, with learning difficulties was developing her work skills in an office environment and dealing success-fully with all communication needs, even to the point of speaking up at the small team meetings. She had put forward some very useful ideas of how to improve the efficiency of data collection and had been asked to speak on the ideas to a regional meeting. Before the meeting she developed a headache at head office and generally felt ill. It was later ascertained that she had a fear of being in large groups of people. She felt that if she was able to dictate her ideas into a cassette recorder for the meeting or have someone present them, this would allow her to make a contribution. This went very well and video conferencing for all participants is now being considered.

This information can be useful in drawing out past or present circumstances that were notable either for positive or negative reasons. Try to identify why they were notable, e.g. people, environment, activities, independence or lack of it.

Help identify situations in the job-matching process (too noisy, too isolated etc.) that were a problem in the past. Getting some information about why the client wants a job and what would be good about getting a job may help identify potential job markets to investigate.

Information on likes and dislikes can be very informative with regard to the types of environment that may be more appropriate for the client to start work.

See Case Study 3.5

Case Study 3.5

Wendy, a 38-year-old, returned to work after a brain injury following a car accident. Following three different work experiences in a three-month period offered by the DEA, she was referred to a supported employment agency. Wendy identified a job in a small factory setting packing toys as the best work experience she had undertaken. The agency found a similar job in a DIY retail organisation. After two frustrating weeks Wendy didn't like the job. Delving deeper, the job developer realised that it wasn't the work environment that she had liked, it was working with one particular supportive co-worker that had made the job enjoyable. Eventually Wendy chose a food preparation job in a retail store café and the job developer ensured that the employer had a co-worker available who was willing to support Wendy during the first few months. Support is ongoing.

If parents/carers are directly involved in this process, supporting the client, then it would be helpful if they could expand upon the information the client has given. If there is a conflict of information, note down all information and try and consider which is more relevant, using all other information given. If there is still doubt, and it is a fundamental issue, then it may only be resolved by arranging job tasters in different situations.

Parents or other family members could well be the most influential factor in decision-making by the client, so it is unrealistic to ignore their views. Much better would be to get them on board in any development planning. They may be able to support in many ways: local knowledge, past experience of work issues, practical experience of working with the client to get the best out of him or her. They can be powerful advocates for change; on the flip side, they can also be powerful adversaries in developing independence for the client. There could be a range of important reasons for this obstruction: fear for the client in the frightening outside world, fear of loss of income from disability benefits. Don't shy away from these issues; it is best to know what you are up against, the barriers to progression, in order to develop strategies to combat them. The following might help:

- practical examples of individual development successes

- comprehensive benefits advice

- better-off calculations, including access to in-work benefits

- using positive parents as examples

- identifying the need for independent living in the future when family members may not be around, as this can be a powerful incentive.

After all this, it may still not be enough and parental obstruction can lead to failure to secure sustainable employment. Learn and move on.

Now complete Exercise 3.2.

Exercise 3.2

Jenny, who is 31 years old and has learning difficulties, lives at home with her mother, father and sister. Her profile suggests that an office environment would be a good starting point. Her work on a short job taster has been exemplary but her enthusiasm is faltering. There appears to be a problem at home and when her work supporter discusses this with her, she says that her father is always bullying her, devaluing her work and abilities and she spends most of her time alone in her room. Her mother does not help and her sister is never there. Jenny feels she can't be herself at home and that this is affecting her work.

- Consider the potential strategies for helping Jenny overcome this negative situation.
- Who else could you involve?

Educational information/academic skills

Remember, skills developed in a variety of situations not directly related to employment may well indicate abilities to hold down a job in different working environments.

This may be a rather imprecise area from which to glean information, as the client may not have had any formal education for a long period of time, but the information could still be useful, particularly if he or she has had any recent vocational or social skills training. Again, try to elicit information on areas liked/disliked.

Parents/carers or ex-colleagues could be a useful source of information in this area. Identify post-school studies, all sorts of educational experiences may be useful in the job search. Even if not employment-related these may show evidence of skills that will transfer very well into a work situation.

Work experience and other information

It may seem as though we are going over the same ground and getting the same information in different formats, but this can help add depth and weight to the job-match choices agreed with the individual. The different formats may also bring out new information to help you develop a support strategy.

Note down any comments that may indicate particular preferences, earnings, shift work, hours, or potential jobs. These can always be considered later in the process. Try to find out whether the client has any particular jobs in mind and reasons for this choice. A point to be noted here is that the relatively small amount of experience people with disabilities have usually relates to the job their father, mother, brother or sister has. This could mean that they make similar choices not because it fulfils their aims and aspirations but because it is familiar. This can lead to job choices that end in mismatch and ultimately to failure. Look at previous experience, consider alternatives even where there appear to be clear choices. See Case Study 3.6.

Case Study 3.6

We can all recount the apocryphal 'I want to be a pilot' stories but getting beyond that simplistic statement can often lead to very useful information on potential job choices.

Trevor, a 22-year-old with Asperger syndrome, was adamant that he wanted to be a pilot when completing his VP. The job

---

Case Study 3.6 continued

developer arranged a job taster at a regional airport and Trevor walked around looking at the various jobs on offer, restaurant worker, porter, maintenance, and baggage handling. He was clearly drawn to the baggage handling as it involved working in close proximity with aircraft which was what he really wanted. He returned for two more half days and didn't want to leave. He now works in the baggage handling department, operating machinery and motorised trolleys. He is still in exactly the place he wants to be, and is a conscientious, valuable employee.

Now complete Exercise 3.3.

Exercise 3.3

Find two people, colleagues or family, willing to discuss one past job and their present job. Identify three things in their past job they liked and three things they didn't like. Do the same for their present job.

- Are there any similarities?
- How did they resolve their dislikes?
- Did they carry forward their likes from the past job into the present one?

What job would you like to do now?

This is a question that can be answered in some interesting, unusual and surprising ways. The client may have a very clear idea about a particular career path clearly related to his or her skills and experiences, or may only have a simply formulated personal goal. Both extremes offer crucial information for the job developer. In the first case some careful discussion may divulge the fact that this is what others think is best but is not what the individual really wants. In the second case the same careful discussion may indicate a very clear and closely held aspiration that can be developed. The point is not to judge too quickly but to listen carefully and discuss all possibilities so that both you and the client are clear about potential directions to investigate.

Workplace flexibility requirements

We are looking for changes that may be needed for a successful job match. We need to deal with all issues that will require changes or at least some flexibility in working practices on the part of the employer so that there are no 'surprises' later on.

There may well be changes, as in any employment situation, but we should have made an open and realistic start that will minimise any negative reactions when negotiation is needed later in the process. Use the client's direct experiences to pinpoint aspects of the working environment that may need examining more thoroughly to ensure that support is adequate.

See Case Study 3.7.

Case Study 3.7

Karen, a 33-year-old with a profound hearing impairment, had just the right computer skills for an employer that was working in the IT field. However, the office of six people was not well suited to someone with a hearing impairment. Having consulted Karen and co-workers, a major office reorganisation was undertaken to enable Karen to communicate effectively. This change not only supported Karen but had a very positive effect on all staff and was found to benefit all office users.

Although this is considered later in the profile, in the employee skills/preferences grid, try to draw out any additional information or areas that the employee feels are important, particularly relating to the working environment. Has past experience led them to feel that certain situations are more problematic than others, e.g. use of stairs, certain machinery, dusty atmospheres?

HABITS, ROUTINES, TEMPERAMENT

If the client likes a cigarette with her coffee break but is in a non-smoking environment, or a client talks incessantly about his favourite football club, or another talks loudly, then these issues will have to be faced and solutions found. It doesn't necessarily mean that you have to 'educate' these individuals out of these habits, you just need to be creative in your job search, e.g. find/arrange a smoking area; make sure co-workers have an interest in football; find a noisy workplace where talking loudly is the norm.

PHYSICAL/HEALTH/MOBILITY NEEDS

Are there any changes needed at work to take into account physical or health issues? Think about what should be taken into account, e.g. ability to lift, use of hands, endurance, preference for part-time work, type of working environment, need for close support. To support the client effectively you need to ensure that you get a clear picture of all aspects of the work environment that might cause him or her difficulty.

BEHAVIOURAL CHALLENGES

This is a difficult area but one that needs to be addressed, e.g. does the client have difficulties relating to members of the opposite sex, or if put under pressure does the client 'blow-up'? Why? Is it caused by boredom, frustration, isolation, being devalued? Are there issues around inappropriate behaviour. Are there any emotional difficulties in team or one-to-one situations? See Case Study 3.8.

Case Study 3.8

Malcolm, a young man with learning difficulties and a quick temper when he feels he is being harassed or challenged, wanted to work in a pub restaurant. This was probably not the most ideal (i.e. stress free) environment that could have been chosen, given Malcolm's temper. However, he and the employer agreed to undertake a probationary period to see how it would work out.

The first week was a considerably high learning curve for both Malcolm and the employer and nearly ended in termination because the strategies in place – a set rota, one supervisor who acted as a mentor for any problems, specific job tasks – did not appear to be working. Malcolm walked out in a temper after three days when asked to do a job that that was on his task list but scheduled for a different time. The employer accepted some responsibility for this but Malcolm was told in straightforward terms that walking out was an unacceptable response.

The strategy was changed for the following two weeks with Malcolm 'shadowing' a co-worker who used the rota set for Malcolm. This proved to be a great success because Malcolm saw a co-worker doing the same tasks, having the same hassle and needing to be flexible in the jobs he had to do. The co-worker

Case Study 3.8 continued

handled the situation in a calm and cheerful way that Malcolm began to emulate and situations that would have caused a problem previously were handled well. On the one occasion during his period that Malcolm started to lose his temper he was told by the co-worker to get his act together because everyone worked as a team. This had a profound effect on Malcolm who had never been part of a 'team' before and began to enjoy the experience. It did not stop him getting frustrated or needing to let off steam but he managed it differently, by talking about issues with the supervisor (who worked in a proactive way, trying to anticipate problems) and

It is now established that challenging behaviours usually represent a challenge to services rather than problems intrinsic to the individual. 'Challenging behaviour' is a term reserved for those behaviours that are dangerous or significantly interfere with their life or the lives of others (Pimm 1997). It is also fair to say that in the main we are going to face inappropriate behaviour rather than challenging behaviour in supported employment services. We will need to consider the context in which the behaviour is exhibited as the same behaviour may not be inappropriate in a different setting, e.g. bad language or shouting. Careful discussion may bring out some information about why the behaviour occurs and in what situations this is likely to happen. Advocates, parents or support workers may be able to help here as well. See Case Study 3.9.

Case Study 3.9

A user of day services branded 'unemployable', for many years exhibited such antisocial behaviour – violence to other users, setting fire to property, taking mechanical property to pieces and other abusive behaviours – that he was permanently accompanied by a 'minder' when in the day centre. On first working with an employment adviser, he began to show that he had skills and communication abilities that could be used in a working environment. Having developed a job for him in the local authority machinery maintenance department it was found that far from being unemployable, none of the behaviours exhibited in the day service ever showed themselves in work and he became indispensable in stripping down complex machinery and carrying out maintenance. He is still employed in this job as a valued member of staff.

This also has important implications for referring agencies as it should indicate the need for open and honest disclosure of any disturbing behaviours shown by clients that could result in a risk of harm to themselves and others. Histories of sexual abuse, intimidation, aggression or other violent behaviours should be subject to disclosure by the referring agency and your service should consider very carefully the referral policy that is instituted to cover such eventualities.

If this is identified as an issue then the first stage should be, possibly in conjunction with professionals in the NHS or social services, an assessment of the problem behaviour and factors that contribute to it being exhibited. What are the facts? Are they based on reliable information? What is the exact nature of the behaviour and when does it occur? What is the risk of it occurring in a work environment?

It should be clear that you are establishing a relationship between your two customers, the client (potential employee) and employer, and disclosure about a potential risk to either party needs to be carefully considered. If there was a potential risk in a new job you would feel it necessary to inform the client. The same information must be given to the employer when the risk is considered sufficiently high and will affect the employment situation. How this is done to avoid premature termination of the negotiations to develop a job opportunity will need careful consideration. You will need to:

- consider what the potential risk is and how it could develop

- formulate intervention strategies where appropriate, possibly using extra support

- develop the client's coping strategies for dealing with the problem

- help the client and employer to identify and cope with situations that could cause distress and inappropriate behaviour

- incorporate the knowledge and expertise of other professionals in order to develop appropriate levels of support

- ensure that the client's expectations are clear and unambiguous

- consider staged disclosure to the employer over a set probationary period, depending on the type and seriousness of the behaviour.

Whatever you decide there should be a clear, formal strategy involving accurate information, advice from professional colleagues and a policy on disclosure when the behaviour is disturbing enough to warrant it. Open, honest and frank negotiation with both client and employer may lead to a lost job opportunity but hiding relevant information from either party almost certainly will, with the added negative impact on your service being perceived as unprofessional and untrustworthy.

Employee skills/preferences

The grids in the vocational profile and job analysis forms are not objective measures of preferences; there are individual subjective issues that will be involved. It could be argued that the grids are too simplistic, but they should be seen as a good starting point in engaging both the client and employer (in the corresponding job analysis grids) in understanding the need to get a good job match in developing a long-term relationship. It is also important in getting both client and employer to realise that they play the central roles in the job development strategy.

What we are looking for are guidelines that can be discussed as and when job matches are found. No one indicator will be significant, but there will be some important characteristics that either show that the match is going to be easy or that it will be problematic. There are identical grids in the job analysis form for the employer to complete, and the comparison should help focus on particular issues that need addressing or accommodating before work experience is considered.

The grids (see Appendix 3 for partially completed examples) identify the closeness of the match by checking key environmental and job-specific characteristics. Use the boxes to score the employee preferences and skills.

- A mark in box 1 indicates a clear preference for the statement on the left of the scale.

- A mark in box 9 indicates a clear preference on the right of the scale.

- A mark in box 5 indicates no preference or average skill in that area.

- Add any skills/preferences to the list that the client feels are relevant.

- Add any narrative on the grid or continuation sheet that will offer clarity and help with the matching process.

If there are differences in the client's needs and the employer's job characteristics we need to:

- identify those that will not have any effect on the job match, e.g. the client exclusively wants full-time employment and the employer has no preference

- identify those that need to be resolved by either the client or employer, e.g. the client needs to get to work at a set time or the employer needs to rearrange the job tasks

- make changes in order to close the 'gap' between client skills and job needs.

Now complete Exercise 3.4.

Exercise 3.4

John completed the employee skills/preferences grid shown in Appendix 3. He has cerebral palsy, which affects his walking abilities. He is 20 years old and has never worked. His preferences are based on a short work experience course he did two years previously. Plasmides Ltd was the employer that completed the corresponding job characteristics/requirements grid in Appendix 3. It is a large company; this grid was undertaken in the warehouse department.

Consider the two grid sections in Appendix 3 and examine the gaps or mismatches in the client's preferences and the job requirements.

- Are they significant? Why/Why not?
- What strategies could you use to try to close the gaps?

Support needs checklist

This is based on past or current experience with the client having a very clear idea of his/her own support needs. Identified needs should be approached in a positive way, that is, we need to know the client's opinion in order to try and get a suitable job match. It is not about excluding someone because his or her needs are difficult to meet. In discussion with the client you may perceive previously unidentified needs; note these down and come back to them in further discussions in order to clarify whether they are accurate.

You may well have identified issues from the information already gathered and some pertinent questioning may help elicit whether the client needs full support, some assistance or is completely independent in any specific area.

Use your knowledge of other service providers to offer advice and information on any aids and adaptations that could support the match in particular situations. See Case Study 3.10.

Case Study 3.10

Brendan, a man of 38 with learning difficulties, finds it difficult to follow a list of instructions, whether spoken or written down. The employer had been used to giving instruction at the start of a job and letting the employee get on with it. A job supporter was employed to work alongside Brendan. Together they went through the whole job and discussed any problem areas. The job was broken down into separate tasks and Brendan was given one task at a time, noted on a simple job card, that also had a picture of the task on it. In this way, it was found that Brendan could complete each individual job task, once shown, without any difficulty. Brendan still has difficulty multi-tasking but is able to carry out the jobs now without a job supporter by using a job card index that means he can take each one out in order, complete the task and put the card back in the box.

For another person with a similar difficulty a cassette recorder was used, for another a white board and marker pen.

Personal disability information

This information is to inform the job-seeking process and therefore only medical details relevant to that process are needed. When completing the 'Other relevant health information' section, it would be useful to ask if the client has any other relevant conditions and what effect these may have in relation to work activities. Prompts could be given if necessary to clarify the information.

Ask the client how he or she would describe the disability and its effect, relating this clearly to employment. We are not interested in medical minutiae but in any evidence of support needs in the workplace.

- Has a diagnosis been discussed with you?

- If you need to take medication, do you need help or privacy?

- Does your condition affect your mobility, concentration, hearing etc.? If so, how?

- What changes can you suggest?

- Do you have any other conditions that could have an impact on an employment situation?

If there are some concerns expressed by either you or the client about the impact of the disability in an employment situation then it may be advisable to seek professional advice from a GP or relevant consultant. See Case Study 3.11.

Case Study 3.11

A young man with cerebral palsy, well supported by parents, began to look for a full-time job. He approached a supported employment agency and, having completed a profile and agreed that an office administration environment would be a good starting point, an interview was arranged at a local financial services office. The interview was successful and there were some changes made – a suitable chair, rearrangement of the office and computer adaptations. After one week, the employer contacted the supported employment agency quite angry that they had not informed him about the fact that the young man had epilepsy, and he had had a seizure in the office. Fortunately, the supervisor had a sister with epilepsy and had dealt with it quite easily. The family had not told the supported employment

Case Study 3.11 continued

agency about the epilepsy as they felt it would have an adverse effect on the young man getting a job. If the supervisor had not had the experience of dealing with epilepsy then the non-disclosure would likely have had the same effect. If the employer had not managed the situation and had withdrawn from the arrangement then it would not only have affected the young man but also any future contact with that company, and the reputation of the agency would have been damaged. The young man is still with the same company.

Whilst this is a sensitive area and, because of employer ignorance or fear, has led to discrimination, it is imperative that we ascertain all disability and medical information that is likely to have an impact in a working environment if we are going to ensure that support is available in an effective way.

Benefits information

Again, this is a very sensitive and complex area and can be a major cause of employment failure for people with disabilities. Any change in benefits has an effect not just on the clients themselves but also on their families, particularly if the family are carers and rely on that income.

However, it is very important to get an accurate picture of a client's income, as this will have a major effect on any decision about employment. If there is any doubt, permission needs to be sought to contact the Benefits Agency, parent, carer, advocate etc. (ensuring that the client has given written permission for contact to be made). *Get expert advice.*

The decision to actively seek employment for people with disabilities is a very courageous one, given the implications it can have on family relationships and income. It is therefore right and proper that the client has all the relevant information available before making such a decision.

- Will I have less money if I get a job?

- Will I lose all my benefits?

- Will I be able to work part-time?

- Will I have to pay for transport?

- Will I have a better quality of life, even with less income?

- Will I have a better social life?

- Will I be making a contribution in a job?

- Will I gain in self-confidence?

- Will I learn new skills and gain experience?

- Will I be able to move jobs, gain promotion?

- Will I be able to get my benefits back if it doesn't succeed?

There are powerful, emotive decisions to be made that are, despite our personal opinions, the sole responsibility of the client. We need to ensure that we offer support, accurate information and advice in order for the client to make informed decisions. *Get expert advice.*

Stick to the information that a job developer might reasonably be expected to gather; identify potential eligibility for Disabled Persons Tax Credit (DPTC). Keep updated a number of benefit examples that illustrate the potential income for people in a range of circumstances. You may be able, in the straightforward cases, e.g. a single person living at home with no housing costs, to work out a reasonably accurate assessment but always *get expert advice* before a final decision is made. See Case Study 3.12.

Case Study 3.12

David, a 28-year-old wheelchair-user (he had suffered a spinal injury) had been out of work for five years and was on a high level of benefits. He was desperate to get back into work but his mother was very obstructive and felt that he wouldn't be able to cope and would also be worse off financially. David persisted and using supported employment found work in a factory making machine castings. Whilst he was indeed worse off financially (by £10 per week), David felt that being with co-workers and earning a living was worth the price, given his improved emotional well-being and greater confidence.

You need to encourage the client to consider the broad consequences of getting a job, not just whether it will make the client financially better off now, but also the financial consequences if he or she returns to benefits later on. There is little point in collecting, or trying to collect, the vast amount of information relating to resources if you will need to refer the client on to a benefits specialist. It is probably more useful to tackle the broad issues around benefits and return to work with some relevant examples drawn from real situations so the client will have information that will help him or her make a choice about the future.

Information analysis/review

Complete a summary of all the relevant information and the basis on which you will be advising the potential employee. Use the information gathered to help the client consider all viable options and make choices. If the choices are within the range of potential development opportunities that the service is capable of delivering, then proceed. If, however, the choices made are outside these parameters, then you will need to acknowledge this and support the person to access an appropriate alternative service, e.g. further education, voluntary work, therapeutic earnings etc. See Case Study 3.13.

Case Study 3.13

Steven, a 32-year-old man with cerebral palsy, has high support needs. He lives in a flat and uses direct payments to buy in his own support workers. He attends a computer course at a Further Education college one day a week, he is on the committee of a local advocacy voluntary group and he runs a website offering advice to people with disabilities. He also wanted to work! Having completed a vocational profile he had to face the reality of having to earn enough to cover his needs and the fact that he would have to reduce his other commitments. He eventually decided against work and increased the time spent on voluntary concerns.

If agreement is reached on a way forward then note down what actions you, the client, the DEA and any other relevant person are going to take in the job-finding process. These actions are then noted in part one of the Development Plan that with the vocational profile is copied for the client. See Appendix 4a for an example of this form.

Maintaining the profile after a job is found

As already stated the vocational profile is the information base in a constantly developing process and as such should be updated on a regular basis as circumstances, preferences and aspirations change. It is a natural process of learning new skills, outgrowing work environments, jobs changing over time due to many reasons – and the profile needs to keep up with these changes.

The profile is part of the overall development strategy and will, throughout the client's employment, need to be assessed in relation to the job analysis and the ongoing support review in order to ensure the progression plan is on track.

The progression plan may well be one that is geared towards progression into open employment or it may be in place to ensure that the client maintains his or her employment as it stands. In either situation, it is important that the support review is completed thoroughly in order to ensure that the client is being supported in the most effective way possible.

You may well get resistance from either the employer or client who might see little point in a review if things don't change. You will have to explain that the purpose is to ensure that you are providing an appropriate service and there are always changes that need to be considered.

If you fall into the trap of believing that clients always need supported employment and the status quo is in their best interests then you will have failed them. You may well miss opportunities to support clients in developing more positive working situations and further extend their employment or even achieve open employment. See Case Study 3.14.

Case Study 3.14

Joan, a young woman with learning difficulties, was taken on by an employer with the support of a supported employment service. The packing duties she was given were limited to supporting a team of co-workers, as Joan was considered to be too slow and nervous to work in the production line. The employer was content to continue the arrangement as Joan was a good worker within her 'limitations' and Joan was content as she was earning a full wage. The job developer, however, was not content as he felt that there was much more that Joan could give. After some months discussing the issue with both client and employer a development plan was agreed and Joan began to work in other departments. It was found that Joan had hidden skills in ensuring that the contents of the packing boxes were counted and coded correctly, a difficult problem to solve that led to high return rates. Joan is now working in open employment as a checker on the production line. This has led to increased bonuses for all her co-workers as well!

Exercise 3.5

Find a willing victim(!) and undertake a full vocational profile, collating all the information on a copy of the form in this book (see Appendix 2a). Discuss the completed form with the 'client' and agree a plan of action for their future job development. Complete the review.

- Was it a positive experience, both for the 'client' and yourself?
- Did the 'client' feel included in the decision-making process?
- Did a possible strategy for development begin to be drawn out?

Ongoing monitoring of the profile

The effects of changes, or incidents, e.g. job technology changes, a valued co-worker leaving, ambitions changing, or (more seriously) being abused at work, can cause stress or problems in a variety of ways that affect job performance. Monitoring the vocational profile and how these issues affect the development strategy needs to be taken into account. Try to spend some time on the details of the vocational profile at each visit and this will then feed into the overall support review.

It is important that a review date is agreed. This date would usually be after a period of between three and six months, as appropriate to the client and assessor. It is important to realise that this is a 'living' document and should take into account individual development and be updated in line with changing experiences and preferences. We all move along and change our minds and the profiling process should accommodate this in its review procedure. This date will vary according to the individual situation and may well coincide with employer timetables. Try to ensure that it is not seen as conflicting with the natural course of events at the worksite. This may be unavoidable and should be approached sensitively. You do have a responsibility to carry out the development plan, as it is important both for the client and your overall service development.

Job tasters

It will be useful to discuss the potential need for job tasters when there is confusion around individual choice or lack of knowledge in an area of interest.

It is important to note that job tasters are not like work experience schemes, they are not long-term nor do they teach how to do a job. They provide an opportunity to gain knowledge of a particular working environment in order to make a job choice based on that practical experience. They can last a couple of hours or even a couple of days; only under exceptional circumstances should they last more than a week. It can help a great deal to eliminate a list of previous work choices as being undesirable just as it can to identify more work possibilities. Job tasters are not essential for all clients prior to employment, but if they are undertaken the clients should be adequately supported in order to get the most out of them.

Job developers need to get a clear picture of the relevant factors in any preferences shown. It may be the work environment, the work itself, the co-workers or the distance from home, or a combination of all these. Reasons for rejection of any experience also need to be examined. Are they the same reasons already noted, or is it rejected because of training methods, personal support environments or again a combination of these? All details will help in finding appropriate work.

If your relationship with current employers is a positive one then access their support in the job taster plan. If they are unable to support they may have other contacts that could be 'encouraged' to offer some time.

You may be able to use the DEA to arrange job tasters but make sure the nature of the taster is understood by the client, as his or her previous experience would have been with work experience schemes.

The client may well have particular local employers in mind and whilst cold calling is probably the most difficult and least successful method of developing an employment situation, it can help.

Conclusion

Vocational profiles should help clients recognise what they have achieved in life, to identify their preferences and the skills they have gained through experience. For job developers it should give a clearer picture of the client's interests, preferences and aspirations, enabling them to help the client make choices and identify a job development strategy that will contribute to a good job match. It is far too easy to underestimate the importance of initial and ongoing assessment and of ensuring that the individual is at the centre of this process. It is important to reflect upon the fact that people may well be the best assessors of their own needs and of how to arrive at solutions for fulfilling those needs. Assessments, then, should focus on those needs and on strengths and experiences of the client in their everyday lives.

However, the vocational profile process doesn't sideline the employer's needs, as it must be clearly matched by an analysis of the job and conditions that the potential employee will need to work under.

What the process does is attempt to match potential employee and employer in a more organised and effective way, trying to deal with issues in a open and proactive way, which can only make the match more efficient and long-lasting, with a greater potential for unsupported employment in the future.

Chapter 4

Job Search and Marketing

Job-finding

If part one of the Development Plan results in your service supporting the client to find work, you then begin the search. You will need to marshal all resources, including DEAs, family and friends, to help find and develop appropriate contacts that can lead to a job.

Job developers help to find jobs that best match the preferences of clients. Using their knowledge of the local job market and by using other services the job developer acts in a facilitating role, as the 'eyes and ears' of clients, assessing potential job matches.

You are going to have to be more attuned to the job market. You will have to ensure that the individual has the support to present the best possible case to any potential employers. Let us take a closer look at the two partners in this enterprise – the employee and employer – and see how your support can be made more effective.

The client/employee

There are four main areas for the client to consider before beginning an employment search.

PRESENTATION

- Does the client understand the need for his or her appearance to be appropriate to the type of job chosen?

- Does the client care about appearance? If not, why not?

- Will this impact on the type of job the client is able to go for, irrespective of his or her skills or experience?

It is not supportive to ignore this aspect if there is a concern that it will adversely affect the client's chances of finding an appropriate job. Make the client aware of the issues and then let him or her make the choice.

Now complete Exercise 4.1.

Exercise 4.1

Phil is 42 years old and has dyspraxia. He works as an administration clerk in a large public organisation, and feels that he is ready for promotion. He is also a fanatical local club football supporter. He can get very angry if football is discussed and his team is criticised; so much so that his behaviour has caused concern at work. One Monday morning Phil turned up at work with a skinhead haircut, wearing a new football shirt from his local club and trainers. The manager is concerned about his appearance.

- How do you approach this whole issue? Is it an issue?
- What plan of action would you put into place if you felt this should be sorted out?
- Should Phil be told there is a problem? If so, how?

When you have considered this and written down your responses, look at Appendix 10, which is a letter that could have been sent. Is it appropriate? Does it go too far? Use it in discussion with colleagues to draw out their views.

SKILLS AND EXPERIENCE

It is important that you get as much information as possible about any experience the client has in the relevant tasks. This could be in related work situations or extrapolated from other experiences, e.g. hobbies, (outside interests may have given the exact skills that are being called for in the potential job opportunity). You need to ensure that the employer is made aware of this fact. See Case Study 4.1.

Case Study 4.1

Ralph, a 23-year-old with cerebral palsy and learning difficulties, was beginning to look for a full-time job in gardening or nursery work as he had helped his father in his work and developed a broad knowledge of plants and their care. A profile was completed and the job developer began to look for work in local nurseries, large estates and local authority parks. This was not going too well until the job developer, when talking to a friend of Ralph's, was told that Ralph had a passion for wild animals and birds and was a local expert in this field. A local wildlife farm that had work in this area as well as upkeep of the grounds was approached and a job taster was arranged. The farm manager was so impressed with Ralph's knowledge that a job was arranged immediately, with the job developer offering some close support in the initial stages. Ralph or his mother had not mentioned the hobby as they hadn't thought it was relevant.

LOCAL EMPLOYMENT KNOWLEDGE

If the client is recommended by an employee, or knows the employer, this can improve chances of getting a foot in the door. Any connection turns 'a cold call into a warm call' (Bissonnette 1994).

- Family and friends can be vital sources of local work information.

- DEAs have many local connections that could prove useful.

- Develop contacts with the local Chamber of Commerce, small firms organisations or local authority business support units.

POSITIVE ATTITUDE

This is related to the potential interview opportunity and is about presenting the best possible front to the employer. Direct questions about the company and the job show a positive attitude and encourage the employer to believe that the client is committed. Relating the job to past experience also helps, as it gives the employer confidence that the client is capable of fulfilling the needs of the job.

Try to find out any information about the company before an interview and prepare some questions to ask. If the client needs some coaching in asking questions or appears nervous then set up a mock interview and try to draw out the best from him or her.

We will need to support people so they can put forward the most effective image in order to secure a job opportunity. There are also benefits in doing a comprehensive resumé for each person that should help in the job search. Use the vocational profile to condense the information about:

- personal objectives
- education
- experience
- special skills
- hobbies
- references.

Complete these elements with the client, putting them onto the profile analysis sheet, starting with the person's career objective – what do they want to achieve by getting a job? For example:

- To get a job where I can use my skills and experience to be a useful member of the company.
- To use my knowledge and strengths to help others achieve their goals.
- To get a job that will further my career ambitions.
- To earn enough money to become independent.
- To meet more people and develop a more interesting social life.

The employer

You will need to understand the difference between asking for support and offering an employment recruitment service. You are trying to ensure the employer is interested in the client's skills and experience, and how the client can contribute to the employer's purpose.

Most employers understand the need for job matching and if you can offer a service that will get to the heart of this then you will have a better chance of achieving a successful outcome for both client and employer. During the employment of the client you will probably also need to deliver a professional and supportive service so the employer feels part of the development process and not left to sink or swim.

- Have you completed a profile that gives a clear picture to the employer of the skills and experience and needs of the client?

- Have you relevant advice and support for the employer in making appropriate changes to improve the chance of successful progression?

- Can you negotiate from a position of strength? Knowing the client has the skills and experience or the potential to fill the job needs is an important advantage.

- Are you fully briefed and able to tackle any issue that may arise?

If you have the information and experience to answer the employer's concerns you are well on the way to getting the client a job.

It is worthwhile noting that most jobs are not advertised; family and friends through their employer and work contacts find most jobs. It is also important to know that most jobs are found in small companies (1–20 employees). Using current employer contacts – suppliers, competitors, buyers etc. – can be an important route to new jobs. The Training and Enterprise Council (TEC), now the Learning and Skills Council (LSC), or the local Chamber of Commerce may also be of help.

It is important to get clients involved in the job-finding process; this will not only give you an indication of their commitment to finding work but will also keep them informed of all the choices, and they can evaluate their interest as you proceed with the job search.

Looking through local newspapers for potential job ads may help clients choose jobs that will fulfil their needs. A pattern of choice may emerge that may help the job-matching process for both the client and the job supporter. The DEA may well have information about a particular field and should have local knowledge of the job possibilities in general. Other supported employment organisations may be able to help with contacts if you develop a relationship in which you share information without reservation.

Remember the goal is employment success for the client not which agency has the largest contact base. If you have just offered a contact to another agency that proved successful you will not only have a positive relationship with that agency but will have developed a positive relationship with an employer who may well be able to help at a later date or establish a contact with another employer. There will always be other contacts to call upon.

The local newspapers, local authority, social services, disability organisations, local business groups, Rotary Club, Chamber of Commerce, Learning and Skills Councils etc. may have information that could help as can any local member of the

Employers Forum on Disability. Build up a database of companies, contacts and information, as this may help with future job searches.

Complete the Job Finding Form (see the copy in Appendix 5) whenever a firm contact is made. This will not only be useful in getting a picture of the local companies, job opportunities and possible changes, but will help with other clients by building up an employers database. See Case Study 4. 2.

Case Study 4.2

Rose lost her job when the factory closed down. We completed a new profile and discussed job possibilities with the DEA and Rose's parents (with her agreement). A job possibility was identified and Rose completed a job taster. Unfortunately, a road accident left the owner hospitalised and his wife trying to hold on to the company so Rose could not take up employment. However, Rose's father discussed the situation with his employer who knew a company that might fit Rose's expectations. Having made contact and received a favourable response the job developer arranged another job taster to look at any 'gaps' in the workplace support. It proved a good match for both employer and Rose and she is now employed full-time using a supported employment tapered funding agreement.

Now complete Exercise 4.2.

Exercise 4.2

Extrude Plastics has a job on offer for a full-time worker in its finished parts preparation and packing department. This is a new job to cope with increased work. The person will need to work in a small team sharing all the jobs. The finished parts, ten in all (but only three parts made on any one shift), need to be checked for defects in three different areas: cracks, extrusion flanges still on the part and misshapes. Checking for these defects is a high priority as whole batches will have to be returned for checking, costing a lot in transport

Exercise 4.2 continued

and irritating customers. Packing is carried out pre-lunch and last thing in the afternoon ready for despatch.

Michael has only worked part-time before but has some packing experience working at a wooden toy manufacturer. He can count up to ten but has problems with larger numbers. He is very methodical in his work but prefers one task at a time before moving onto another task. He does have difficulty remembering the right task procedures and gets confused if left alone for any length of time. He is very conscientious and likes to make sure everything is done correctly which is why he gets frustrated if he makes mistakes.

Your task, having arranged an appointment to see the employer with Michael is to develop a negotiating pitch that will convince the employer that Michael is just right for the job. Anticipate possible barriers and rejection issues by 'selling' the person and their skills rather than the support you offer.

Remember you are the catalyst not the glue.

Person-centred Planning (PCP) and the traditional job market

It is fair to say that the regular approach to filling a job – the employer identifies a range of tasks that need doing, draws up a job description and job specification, advertises for applicants, interviews them and offers the job to the best (in their eyes) applicant – doesn't make for a successful conclusion for most people with disabilities.

People with disabilities, particularly severe disabilities, are unlikely to be able to fill a job using a standard job description, even with accurate matching and aids and adaptations. See Case Study 4.3.

If we were to be honest, the traditional approach to job filling suits very few people; everyone would prefer his or her individual skills and experiences to be considered individually rather than be measured against a group of other job applicants.

I am not advocating moving the emphasis away from filling employers' needs to only filling potential employee needs, but both 'customers' are important in the job-matching process (that is what all job filling is about) and giving this full consideration will be more beneficial for both the employer and employee in the long term.

Case Study 4.3

A large retail store declared itself to be positive about employing people with disabilities and ensured that at least 15 per cent of applicants for the jobs in a new store were people with disabilities. They held the interviews on the first floor of their administration building accessible only by stairs, had questionnaires to complete only in writing and, whilst accepting a person with a hearing impairment for interview, would not allow a BSL translator to attend. They also said that all applicants must be able to complete all the different duties to enable them to have a fully flexible workforce! The word 'flexible' was in no way used ironically.

You will need to work hard to transform the situation so that people with disabilities can present themselves in terms of their individual skills and the contribution they can make to fill the employer's identified need. Negotiating employment opportunities in this new way presents us with the classic 'win–win' situation. Employees find jobs that meet their aspirations and skills and employers have job vacancies filled effectively but creatively.

Employers implicitly understand the need for such an approach, as there are innumerable instances of costly failures in trying to fit an apparently suitable successful interview applicant into a job only to find that the match is less than successful.

You are not overselling the client but you are saying that you understand the need for an effective match and will offer advice and support to achieve this and gain sustainable employment for people with disabilities in the process.

Marketing

Marketing our supported employment service is about finding jobs for our job-seekers. We can, therefore, define marketing as: '... the management process responsible for identifying, anticipating and satisfying consumers' requirements profitably' (Cheshire County Council 1997, Module 3, Topic 1, p.13).

This part of the supported employment process has two main purposes: one is to market the service and the other is to market the particular individual.

When marketing the service and to develop it effectively you will need to look at marketing it to the major players: people with disabilities and employers.

In the job-finding stage of marketing we focus on the employer. For job developers to work effectively at job-finding they need to understand the local market they are working in: what are the local industries, who are the local employers, where are the job openings? A good starting point is the vast amount of research in the area of employer needs. Employers are looking for:

1. Dependability

2. Low absence rate

3. Low turnover rate

4. Industriousness

5. Independence

6. Speed

7. Accuracy

8. Job knowledge

9. Image

10. Social interactions

(Cheshire County Council 1997, Module 3, Topic 1, p.18)

You need to find out what kind of mix of these qualities local employers are looking for. See Case Study 4.4.

Case Study 4.4

Maggie had a visual impairment, which meant she tackled job tasks methodically and slowly. The job developer looked at a range of local companies and found one, a machine reclaiming factory, that had a reputation for needing quick and accurate workers. He went to the job prepared to negotiate on the quick and emphasise the accurate. However, he found that the company was desperate for someone who would perform two particular tasks, which reclaimed expensive parts as accurately as possible. All current workers tried to be quick and damaged too many of the parts. Maggie fitted in very well, reducing the damage to almost nil and able to reclaim all the parts economically even at a reduced speed.

It will be clearly impractical for a job developer to know everything about employment situations in the locality and you should organise your networking as effectively as you can. For instance, the DEA will have local knowledge and ways of obtaining information that will be invaluable in focusing in on any particular area that has been identified by your client. You need to ensure that the DEA presents supported employment in a way that best underlines your provision. You should support DEAs with appropriate publicity material and liaise regularly to keep the information current. You will, however, need to get specific information and look at what your own resources are in order to achieve a positive outcome.

When dealing with a client you will have to be able to change the focus of your marketing strategy to suit individual needs.

- Is the client's interest restricted to a particular geographical area?

- Does he or she wish to work in a specific industry, retail, factory, farming etc.?

- Are certain working conditions preferred?

See Case Study 4.5.

Case Study 4.5

Mick, a supporter of his local football club, has a lifetime season ticket. This meant that Saturdays were sacrosanct and he wouldn't work. This proved a difficult problem as his preferred work was in a local supermarket that opened all day on Saturdays. After protracted negotiations, it turned out that the store actually needed 'rumblers', people who would come in after store closures and restock the shelves ready for the next day. This was usually in fairly anti-social hours and staff were reluctant to work. The store had a policy that all staff work Saturdays. This was relaxed for Mick, as he was willing to do the restocking after store hours whenever the store needed and at short notice. Both parties made changes and were happy with the arrangement.

You will then need to develop information-collection strategies that enable you to collate very detailed information on employers in the specific area needed. All employers are different; even from within the same industry there will be significant differences in how companies operate.

You therefore need to look at developing a flexible structure that can:

- undertake qualitative and quantitative research

- forecast future market demand for your 'product' – your service and client

- find the right job – satisfy the needs of both your main customers.

You will have to become more proactive. You also need to establish what the employer's objectives are and how the client's skills will fit into that organisation as employers want people who fit into their organisation and help achieve the company objectives. Vocational profiling and the job analysis will, therefore, be a crucial part of any marketing strategy.

Establishing a relationship with the employer

Establishing a positive relationship with employers will help ensure that it is a long-term one, and that the employer will be more likely to:

- make changes to support needs that arise later in the relationship

- look upon the relationship as mutually beneficial

- deal with the client in an equitable way

- begin to generally view employing people with a disability in a positive way

- advocate the use of your service to other employers.

You will need to make sure the employer sees that you are supporting individuals with the skills and qualities the employer needs. You should also have a clear understanding of four important characteristics of good relationships:

1. Mutual benefits – it doesn't need to be the same benefit but there have to be gains for both parties.

2. Clear roles and expectations – say what you do and do what you say, facilitate the development of the employee/employer relationship.

3. Trust – deliver what you promise and don't offer the moon.

4. Good communication – listen, understand and respond effectively. (Cheshire County Council 1997, Module 2, Handbook, p.11)

Here are some examples of ways in which good relationships can be developed:

- Arrange formal appointments and keep them.

- At the start outline exactly what your service provides.

- Complete a job analysis to understand the job and the employer's job needs.

- Collate all employee/employer details onto a database specifically designed for the purpose and review on a regular basis.

- Agree a support structure and identify natural supports.

- Advise on the use of aids and adaptations and liaise with other service deliverers.

- Draw up a written agreement based on the negotiation process.

Information material

Information material about your service must be used to great effect and can make a big impression on both client and potential employer.

- Does your organisation care about the people it deals with?

- Do you hide behind the use of jargon?

- Do you offer a professional service?

Look at some of the elements for developing a professional service and see how your organisation measures up.

- Agency name – Is it obvious what you do? Does it present a caring and professional image?

- Informational material – Does it say what you do? Is it jargon-free? Does it reflect the principles on which your service is based?

- Front-line staff – Are they trained? Are they able to communicate with clients and employers? Can they negotiate effectively? Do they represent the principles of your service effectively?

- Service language – Is it clear and unambiguous? Does it represent what your service can provide accurately?

- Advertising – Do you have regular ads in the local press? Do you publicise your success stories? Do you have video footage of how the service works or how people are getting on with their lives using your service?

- Never underestimate the problems that arise in running your service.

- Never overestimate the service we can deliver.

- Don't interfere in the day-to-day local support arrangement – understand that the development of a relationship between the employer and employee is vital for long-term stability. This is a difficult area as problems may develop that closer contact could have resolved more easily, but experience has shown that the rewards of waiting for a natural resolution is worth the extra time.

- Always be available for advice.

- Always believe that the employee wants to be seen as a fully integrated employee and all visible differences should be kept to a minimum.

- Have a realistic attitude and do not hang on to an obviously unworkable situation.

- Review customer satisfaction and need in a formal way, particularly at times of change and development. What is the point of having a high quality service available if it doesn't actually fill anyone's needs?

Establishing your credibility as a supported employment service, with both clients and employers, will take time and effort and these are just some of the variables that will make a difference. If you want to develop a sustainable service then you need to consider all these issues continuously. Look at your service and ask the question:

Does our service do what we say it does, does it fulfil the aims of supported employment and is it what is needed to support people with disabilities into open employment and lead inclusive lives?

Negotiating

Having begun to establish a rapport with the employer we can look at the negotiation: 'landing' employment for the client.

Your negotiation will have two sides: one is marketing your organisation as running a successful employment service; the second is focusing on getting a good match between employee and employer. Getting this balance right and dealing successfully with all the issues that arise in the negotiation process will get you a long way down the road to establishing a long-term relationship between employee and employer.

'Flying by the seat of your pants' can be an effective strategy in the negotiating process and can lead to some innovative and successful relationships. It can also lead to emphasis being placed on your service and away from the employee–employer match. Self-belief is good, as is emphasising the quality of your service. However, this will not overcome most problems arising in the course of the support process. The physical support offered by the job developer will be valued highly by many employers, dealing with personnel issues, changes, advice, health and safety issues etc. We also need to recognise that in order to develop a positive relationship between the employee and employer we need to reduce our support to the minimum necessary to achieve success.

The employer will have many skills and natural support mechanisms that can be used to support a person with a disability and many are concerned about equality issues. Be humble about the service you offer, be realistic and rely on the employer as much as possible – they will feel a part of the process rather than just a tool of your service.

Selling and public relations

Consider the following issues when putting your job-finding strategy together.

MARKETING AND NETWORKING

In more commercial environments there could be seen to be a major difference between the 'hard sell' marketing and the more 'touchy feely' networking. For the supported employment field there has always been a more established relationship between the two. However, you need to become much more focused and deliberate in your use of both these strategies.

- Publicise your successes in the employment field.

- Publicise any new developments.

- Develop informative, updated material for wider audiences.

- Build relationships at both local and head office level.

- Reward achievement in employer support for people with disabilities, e.g. by using Employer Award Certificates.

- Use enthusiastic employers to network with more reluctant employers.

SUPPORTED EMPLOYMENT AS A PRODUCT

Be more confident in the service you provide to employers. You are helping them fill vacancies with good employees. You are helping them develop those employees and offering support and advice on a long-term basis – not only to benefit the person with a disability but to help the employer's overall employment policy with advice on health and safety, equal opportunities, disability awareness, the DDA, training development, aids and adaptations, and many other areas that would otherwise perhaps go unsupported or be extremely costly to achieve.

By looking at supported employment as a product you can then begin to see how meeting the needs of your main customers is vital in sustaining a viable service. You will also be able to develop services to meet specific needs and adapt to market changes. You will not be a 'cap in hand' service, reliant upon the charitable nature of employers, but able to meet them on equal terms, supplying them with a service that they value.

USING NETWORKS

Supported employment services have usually been very good at developing networks and working in partnership with other organisations. What they have not been so good at is doing this in a systematic way – developing contacts, adding potential employers to an employer contact list, keeping the information updated and making regular contact.

- How many of you know all the national employers in your area already using supported employment in other locations around the country?

- Could you use people already committed to supported employment to liaise with colleagues in different areas to publicise the positives involved in supporting people with disabilities?

You also need to understand that you may well not be able to offer all the elements of service need and will, therefore, need to liaise with other organisations that can offer that service in order to develop the overall strategy necessary for a successful job match. For instance, there will be cases where a support worker may be necessary to support a particular individual. If you don't have the resources to offer that service yourselves then there may be local agencies that can offer it.

Even if your organisation is small, the use of information technology resources to manage all contacts in a more accessible manner will improve your chances of achieving your aims as well as facilitate liaising with other organisations to help them achieve theirs.

You are not in the business of finding low-grade activities to keep people with disabilities occupied for the daytime or of helping the employers salve their consciences by providing an imitation job. You are there to support people with disabilities in real employment situations, for real money, for real job satisfaction and for real career development.

The skills involved in selling this service and the individual's skills are not alien to the people-centred world of supported employment but are an intrinsic part of developing a successful service.

You need to acknowledge that the wealth of skills and experience developed by you as a job developer in dealing with employers on a wide range of levels, sometimes in difficult circumstances, is second to none. Use this knowledge and experience but don't just work from memory. Use more formal means, e.g. contact forms, full written notes, databases, in order to work proactively to develop new contacts and employment apportunities for people with disabilities.

Potential jobs

Once a potential job has been found, the hardest part is to get a successful closure for the individual. It can be difficult to resist the temptation to offer the world in order to get through the door. This is a dangerous tactic as it invariably backfires when both employer and employee become dissatisfied with the mismatch.

You need to ensure that both parties are very clear about what your service has to offer and the principles underlying the service delivery: (1)inclusion, and (2) progression to unsupported employment. You have started this process with the development of a comprehensive vocational profile for the client and will have discussed the principles of supported employment with both employee and employer. You will need to undertake a job analysis not only to ensure you have a clear picture of the job-match potential but to further convince the employer that their interests are also important. The job analysis is discussed fully in the next chapter but it is an important pre-employment process in order to begin the identification of the job-match potential.

Access to, and use of, appropriate marketing materials will be essential in ensuring that your service is clearly outlined to all parties. The use of employee/employer packs, which could include regular updates about the service provision, individual progression details etc., may be useful.

The negotiation should be based on the profile, supports available and changes that both parties will need to make in order to progress. It is important that any funding strategy is fully discussed and agreed in principle with the employer and employee. Draft agreements could be shown in the packs along with the details of the matching process.

If there is no agreement reached then you will need to return to the job-finding process using other contacts, perhaps refocusing on other areas in light of the negotiations already undertaken. It is important to ensure that clients are fully aware of all details of the process so they can have an input into any possible changes that could help in the next potential job.

If agreement to proceed with the job is reached then the job analysis, already started, can be completed and notes on potential support needs, gaps and changes discussed. Early completion of the job analysis is always recommended to help prevent mismatches at a later stage. It is, however, necessary to make sure that you have the initial agreement of both employee and employer to proceed as you could be in a position of having to undertake a job analysis for every job contact made, which would be impractical and a waste of time.

Now complete Exercise 4.3.

Exercise 4.3

The inevitable and exciting use of role-play!

Organise a role-play with one/two colleagues in which you play the parts of job developer and employer in an initial meeting to examine the possibility of offering an employment opportunity to a person with a learning difficulty. John is 27 years old and has never worked. He has enjoyed some work experience in a large retail outlet but needed close support. He sometimes used inappropriate behaviour in the store when he got over-excited but was always cheerful and was willing to tackle most jobs. The employer should be played showing the greatest reluctance to support the client and the job developer should marshal all arguments and reasons why it would be a positive move.

- What was the outcome?
- What did you learn for future use?
- Were you able to convince the employer?
- Did you use all the reasons possible?
- Were there any areas you could have changed or added to?
- Would you do it differently next time?

Open and honest negotiation and information exchanges may not always save the situation but will ensure that you are confident that you did all that you could to achieve your goal. The least you will get out of this situation is an awareness of any problematic issues that need to be tackled when trying to find another job for the client. Learn and move on.

Chapter 5

Job Analysis

Introduction

Although it is common practice to set out the basic aspects of a job for new recruits, it is not common for all aspects of the job and environment to be examined. People with disabilities are, in general, less familiar with working environments and a lot that would be taken for granted by an able-bodied person could actually be an area where the person with a disability needs some assistance or alteration to working practice.

The main aims of conducting the job analysis (JA) (see Appendix 6a for a copy) are (1), to provide information regarding different aspects of the job in order to gain further evidence about whether the job is likely to match the person's expectations, and (2), to identify aspects of the job with which the person is likely to require specialist assistance. Always consider the job analysis to be 'work in progress', in need of constant refining.

You will have already completed the vocational profile and talked to the client and will therefore be attuned to what may be 'gaps' in the job currently being analysed. Note down, discuss, and suggest possible options right from the start.

Don't be afraid to suggest changes in work environment, hours, ways of working – the employers can only say no, but are more likely to make suggestions of their own.

Keep your mind open to all the possibilities and as you develop a complete picture of the job and working environment, you will understand what may or may not be possible. If practical, you should spend some time visiting the job site, making notes for the JA, rather than relying on the employer or supervisor alone. If this is not practical then make sure you review the job analysis regularly and tackle issues as they arise.

Use the knowledge that supervisors and co-workers already have. Discuss with them the aspects of the job that could cause problems to see if there are alternatives already in place. See Case Studies 5.1 to 5.3.

Case Study 5.1

John went to work in a factory making cardboard templates for the packaging industry. The manager was very enthusiastic and the supervisor already knew John and was happy to support him in developing a range of duties that would suit his needs. The job analysis was completed with the manager, who had worked on the shop floor and 'knew' all the tasks. A particular task involving a machine was felt to be too difficult as it involved four different sub-tasks. John was therefore excluded from this area until, a couple of weeks into the job, the supervisor was talking to the job developer about this. The supervisor laughed, saying that the manager 'knew' the tasks as they were five years ago. He showed John how to use the new machinery, which was much simpler. As a result John has now increased his skill level and performs a greater range of tasks.

We need to gather all the details relating to the job:

- Conditions of employment: hours, wages, other financial benefits.
- Job tasks: core, intermittent and job-related tasks/routines.
- The working environment: physical, social and cultural.
- Health and safety.
- Available support, adjustments needed.

See Case Study 5.2.

Case Study 5.2

Sue began working in a garment factory and was having difficulty with a particular cutting task allocated by the supervisor. The job developer talked to one co-worker who said she had had the same problem until the area was re-organised and the task was done in a different order. She showed Sue how to do it and after a short while the problem disappeared.

Case Study 5.3

Jim began work at a furniture factory making up specialised cloth books for customers. A machine for preparing each piece had been reconditioned and a fail-safe foot control had been installed for health and safety reasons. Jim was unable to use this because he had a mobility problem. This highlighted the fact that none of the other workers could use it properly either, because they needed to move from one end of the machine to the other during the process or had to stretch unsteadily to keep their foot on the control so the machine didn't stop.

There is now a movable hand control, which is just as safe, but all staff can use it properly.

The job analysis form

The following section looks at elements of the job analysis form (see Appendix 6) and offers advice and examples to help complete the details as fully as possible.

Company details

These are the basic details, address, contacts, phone numbers.

Ensure you have full contact details for the company and consider:

- What are their responsibilities?

- What support will they offer to develop the client?

- What is the best way to liaise with them or the direct job supporters?

Job details

Make sure you have the agreed job title and a basic job description or task list. (This can be checked later and details clarified.) If you identify any immediate 'gaps' in either support or tasks that might prove to be difficult then try to draw out from the employer whether there can be changes made to the task list or changes made that would help the client complete the job tasks.

Be open and honest, if you or the client envisage a problem then say so – it may be easily resolved but it may be a major issue and it is best to get it out in the open as soon as possible. The employer will understand this and, hopefully, try to address the issue or you will be able to suggest ways that could alleviate the problem.

WORKING HOURS

This is an important part of the job that can have a major effect on the success or not of the job opportunity.

- Is the job full- or part-time because that is crucial to the company?

- Is it because it has always been full- or part-time?

- Are the hours set because the workload determines this?

- Alternatively, is it because the milk is delivered at 7am?

- Is overtime a necessary part of the job or is it optional?

Negotiate the possibility of change to see how this would affect the employer, supervisor, co-workers, output etc. You will get a good idea of whether there is the chance of a compromise or not and be able to advise the client accordingly, as it may be the client who has to make the change.

PAY RATES

Make sure you have a clear understanding of the pay rates in force in the company for the different jobs and any related bonus, incentive or performance enhancements.

Make it clear that whatever the current conditions are for co-workers in the same job they will also be applicable to your client. A probationary or training period may be customary and you need to understand how this operates and how it will apply for your client. He or she may well be financially out of pocket for this period but if it is understood that in six weeks or three months this will change, it could help the client decide to accept the job. Make sure the client understands the options available and the financial consequences of the decision.

TIMEKEEPING POLICY

There may be a formal system linked to a bonus scheme or there may be an informal system that is monitored by the supervisor. There may be a system of sanctions, loss of pay, and no opportunities to do overtime. Make sure you understand the system in place. If it consists of a one-to-one meeting with the supervisor make sure you know about it and can discuss with the supervisor the effectiveness of such a system in relation to your client and that the client understands the implications of the 'telling off'. See Case Study 5.4.

Case Study 5.4

Jack got his first job aged 42 in a metal fabrication factory working as a packer and warehouse worker. He started well and then after a few weeks began to arrive late, by a few minutes, a couple of times a week. The supervisor took him into the office and told him it wasn't good enough and that he should get to work on time. Jack got visibly upset and went home. The job developer was called in and went to discuss this with Jack. He knew he should get to work on time and didn't have any valid excuse but he felt that the supervisor had singled him out.

'He hasn't told anybody else off for it.' What Jack hadn't understood was that the supervisor told the others off in private as well. When this was explained to him and he understood how important it was to get to work on time there were no more problems. He even began to make a joke of it; whenever people went into the supervisor's office he asked them if they had been 'telled off as well'.

DRESS CODE

What clothing is considered suitable for the environment in which the client is going to be working? It is pointless getting smartly dressed in shirt and tie if you are going to spend the day in a machine shed. Similarly, it is inappropriate to put on dirty overalls if you are working in a front-line reception job. Understand the needs of the job, find out whether working clothes are supplied, either for the whole job or for particular tasks, safety clothing for instance.

Casual clothes to one person may be very different to another. It is unfair to put someone in a situation with which they are not familiar and expect them to understand the nuances of social behaviour, dress codes etc.

As a job developer, it is your job to ensure that the person is fully primed to make the best impression possible. Reconsider Exercise 4.1. This is not to say that there will not be embarrassing moments, but you will help keep them to a socially acceptable level. You may well need to get others to help with this – parents, advocates, friends – in order to reinforce certain behaviours, at least for the first few weeks.

Remember this doesn't just apply to people with learning difficulties; it applies to all those people with disabilities who have not had any experience of working environments and the cultures that go with them. Anyone can struggle in a new social situation before understanding the social etiquette. Job developers are there to help the client reduce those misunderstandings to a minimum.

TRAINING PROGRAMMES

Find out all about the training methods of the employer – is it formal in-house training, external trainers, college courses, 'sitting with Nellie' or a mixture of all these methods? Ensure you understand the methods that might best suit your client and what are the areas that may need explicit training. If these can be accommodated within the employer's system then so much the better, but if they need some alternative methods, see if the company training process can be adapted to fit, or whether extra training can be arranged.

Employers are keen to get appropriately trained workers and if you can help achieve this with an adapted programme then it will more than likely be seen as positive and support will be forthcoming.

COMPANY PENSION SCHEME

- Is there one?
- Is it open to all employees?
- Is it contributory or not?
- Is it a stakeholder pension?
- What are the financial implications for your client?
- What other options are there?

Don't give financial advice to clients unless you are fully qualified to do so. The client will need professional advice in order to make informed choices. Look at the advice available locally and suggest the client seeks appropriate advice from one of the recognised organisations. The employer's pension scheme administrator should be able to offer information about their scheme.

NOTICE PERIOD

- Is the client paid monthly or weekly?
- Is the notice period the statutory monthly or weekly period or is there a different company notice period?
- What are the redundancy conditions?
- Are there formal disciplinary and grievance procedures?

Make sure you get copies of any procedures and ensure they cover all statutory obligations. Make sure the client is aware of the procedures and understands the implications for any future eventuality.

UNION

- Is there a union at the employers?
- If not, are unions recognised?
- If not why not?
- If there is a union, who is the contact?
- Can anyone join?
- Are there any other options?

In general, if there is a union it is recommended that the client join. This will give the client a valuable source of independent advice and support and will ensure the union understands the practice of supported employment. If their members are using supported employment they will feel more positively about the process.

SICK PAY

Get a copy of the statutory sick pay regulations – ensure that this is the minimum the employer allows.

- Is there a company sick pay scheme? What are the terms, e.g. only full-time employees with two years' continuous service, only for sick leave over two weeks, a maximum of 6 weeks in any 12-month period?

This can be crucial for people with disabilities that require regular hospital treatment or have recurring conditions that require rest.

- Is there an informal sick pay scheme at the employer's discretion? If the employer is convinced of the genuine need for leave then the client may get sick pay.

This could make it worthwhile to disclose any condition that could impinge upon the client's job so that the employer can consider the circumstances of the illness. A sudden illness due to a condition that has not been discussed with the employer is not likely to help foster a positive relationship.

HOLIDAYS

Get a copy of the statutory holiday regulations, and ensure these are the minimum applied by the employer.

- Is there a company holiday pay scheme?

- What are the terms? For example, do employees in the first year of service get 1.3 days of holiday for every full month of service? Or do all employees with two years' service get the statutory minimum (pro-rata for part-time employees), employees with three years' service get one extra day, five years' service two extra days and so on?

This can have a big impact on new workers, particularly in the first year when holidays have already been planned. If you know these details from the start, you may well be able to negotiate a compromise with the employer. However, a new worker (and his or her family) will have to realise that there may well be restrictions on the time and number of holidays that were previously taken. There have been cases of the family making holiday arrangements and the client just not turning up for work on a Monday morning with the employer unaware of a reason for the absence. Such a situation can easily lead to dismissal. Remember to ensure that the client and their family, if appropriate, understand the need for accepting the responsibilities along with the rights. If you anticipate this being a problem then it is worthwhile concentrating support on this area until it is understood.

APPRAISAL/DEVELOPMENT PROCEDURE

Whilst you will have a clear development procedure of your own, it is wise to see whether the employer has an appraisal or training development system. Their system will be purely related to job efficiency and the training needs of the individual to fulfil those duties. You have a wider remit, to ensure that the client progresses to open sustainable employment. There may well be agreement between you and the employer but always keeps your eye on the goal and ensure the employer and client understand this. There is no reason why you should not take on board any personal objectives identified in the employer's appraisal and incorporate them into the client's development plan. However, you need to maintain the development plan and not let it be subsumed into the employer's appraisal system.

There is an argument that we should allow this as it makes the employment situation more 'natural' – the same as it is for other employees. The fallacy with this argument is that supported employment is not the same as for the other employees; if it were you would not be around and the client would be openly employed by the employer in exactly the same way as other employees.

The employer's appraisal system may try to incorporate a development plan but usually it will be an annual assessment of how job objectives have been achieved and will set new objectives without considering the overall progression of the employee towards open employment, as it assumes that all employees are in this position already. You need to jumpstart the progression process and make sure it keeps on target.

HEALTH AND SAFETY (H & S)

A crucial area that needs extended consideration and one in which you can judge the employers' respect towards their staff by how much attention they pay towards ensuring staff are safe and well trained in this area.

- Is there a written H & S policy?

- If not, why not? On the face of it, having no written policy can signal a problem, and the matter should be examined more carefully.

However, there are companies who have a written policy but no-one has been trained in its implementation, nor is there an officer responsible for reviewing it. So tread carefully.

- Are H & S assessments carried out?

- By whom?

- What is the impact on working practices? Get to see an assessment and look around the worksite, assessing the state of the place and noting any obvious problems.

See Appendix 7a for a checklist of common H & S issues and Appendix 7b for an entire H & S form, which should be completed for every new job opportunity. It is not exhaustive, but should give you a reasonably clear picture about the worksite, management of H & S procedures and the general working conditions. *Seek expert advice* – The Health and Safety Executive (HSE) will offer comprehensive advice if you have any concerns, and the Local Authority Environmental Health Department will also offer practical advice and give you other contacts if appropriate. There is no harm in asking for advice if you are not sure or concerned about a particular issue.

RISK ASSESSMENT

Risk assessment is a fundamental process for ensuring health and safety in the workplace and is probably the most successful health and safety tool that exists.

The concept of risk assessment is contained in many pieces of legislation. However, whilst other regulations contain similar provisions, such as those for exposure to noise and manual handling, the Management of Health and Safety at Work Regulations 1999 contain the main legislative requirements for employers and the self-employed to carry out assessments.

Employers should assess the risks to all persons affected by their work activities, including non-employees, paying particular attention to those employees who may be at an increased risk such as pregnant women, new mothers, young persons and those with disabilities.

The first step in any risk assessment process is to identify what hazards people may be subjected to. A hazard can be classed as anything that has the potential to cause harm. This can usually be achieved by carrying out a walk-through survey, talking to the people who carry out the work activities.

The second step is to assess the risks. Risk is defined as the likelihood that something will cause harm, together with the severity of injury, from each identified hazard.

Once a work activity has been assessed, a decision has to be made as to whether any existing risk is acceptable. If so, any existing measures used to control the risk must be kept in place. If, however, the risk is unacceptable, additional measures to control the risk must be introduced.

If five or more people are employed, any significant findings of an assessment must be recorded in writing. However, it is recommended that the findings of all assessments be recorded.

Regular checks should always be made to ensure that control measures are being followed. Additionally all assessments need to be reviewed at appropriate intervals to ensure that they are still valid.

Understanding the legislation

Legislative requirement for employers and the self-employed to perform workplace risk assessments initially caused concern and confusion, and to some extent still does, with much mystery being built around the process of assessment. In reality most employers carry out informal risk assessments every day, looking at workplace hazards and deciding what needs to be done to control them.

Risk assessments should, however, be carried out on a more formal basis by searching for all significant workplace hazards, evaluating them in a systematic fashion, recording the findings of the assessments and reviewing them regularly. They can be relatively easy to complete if undertaken in a logical and systematic fashion and should form the basis of an effective health and safety management system. Many ideas and methods are currently in circulation about how to carry out an assessment, varying from crude and simple systems to the extremely complex. According to the needs of the employer each of these systems, evaluating, recording and reviewing, has a place in the process of risk assessment.

It is most important to understand the phrases used in risk assessment as any confusion will lead to that assessment being completed unsatisfactorily. The three phrases that most need to be understood are:

- **hazard** – the potential for something to cause harm, such as electricity, working on a ladder or with dangerous machinery

- **risk** – the likelihood that harm will actually occur from exposure to the hazard, together with the likely injuries that will occur as a result, and the likely numbers of people that this will affect

- **extent of the risk** – the number of people who might be exposed and the consequences for them.

The amount of effort placed into health and safety in the workplace should be based on the risks associated with the work, with the greatest effort being placed into controlling those work activities that create the greater risk. The understanding of the process of risk assessment is therefore crucial to the effective management of health and safety.

There is a wealth of legislation facing employers and the self-employed requiring risk assessments of their work activities to be carried out. The main legislative requirements can be found in the:

- Control of Substances Hazardous to Health Regulations 1999

- Noise at Work Regulations 1989

- Health and Safety (Display Screen Equipment) Regulations 1992

- Management of Health and Safety at Work Regulations 1999

- Manual Handling Operations Regulations 1992

- Personal Protective Equipment at Work Regulations 1992.

Whilst each piece of legislation has its own specific requirements the principles behind all risk assessments are the same and the general guidelines contained in the Management of Health and Safety at Work Regulations 1999 can be used to assist in carrying out more specific assessments under other legislation.

Regulation 3 of the 1999 Regulations requires both employers and the self-employed to:

- carry out a suitable and sufficient assessment of the risks to both employees and others who may be affected by their work activities

- review that assessment when there is reason to suspect that it is no longer valid

- review that assessment when there has been a significant change in the matters to which it relates

- record the significant findings of the assessment and identify any group of employees especially at risk.

The primary purpose of the risk assessment therefore, is to determine what measures need be taken to comply with an employer's duties under health and safety legislation. Records of assessments only need to be made where there are five or more employees.

Understanding the general principles of risk assessment

There are several general principles applicable to risk assessments that should be understood by those undertaking them which apply to all risk assessments, including those required by other legislation.

Risk assessments should be carried out to identify the hazards arising from work activities that employees and other people are exposed to and will be far more successful and less time consuming if well thought-out in advance with consideration being given to what activities form the basis of the assessment. Activities can be divided into:

- individual work tasks
- individual processes
- individual or groups of persons
- by section or department
- generic assessments
- a combination of the above.

Whatever is decided is down to individual preference, although basing the assessment on individual work tasks is generally preferable as it will give a more comprehensive coverage of work-related hazards. Such an approach is often combined with undertaking the assessments on a departmental basis.

Any person planning to undertake an assessment will need to ensure that he or she is competent to do so. If, as they usually are, assessments are carried out in-house there may be occasions where expert help is required. In such circumstances this should be identified at an early stage so that any necessary action can be taken. It is always advisable to start the process of assessment on some potentially low-risk activity until the process and the scoring system have become familiar.

Risk assessments can often form the basis of a system of safe working procedures that can be linked into a company H & S policy statement.

Generic assessments

Risk assessments should be specific to an individual company and its work activities and, wherever possible, site-specific to ensure that all risks are adequately assessed at each work location. However, if work activities are similar across sites, a generic risk assessment covering activities on a group basis, may be a more useful and less time-consuming option.

This could take the form of assessing a group of similar activities, such as cleaning or office work, or assessing a single activity that occurs at several locations. A single or small number of assessments could be undertaken and the results of that assessment then be applied across a company's activities.

Undertaking generic assessments has advantages in that less time is spent assessing similar activities; conversely, it does mean that a greater amount of time has to be spent planning assessments, and additionally there is also the possibility that little or no variation may be made for local working arrangements or situations, so making the process inflexible or open to misinterpretation.

If generic assessments are to be used, they must be valid for the work activities to which they apply and therefore, in order to achieve this, the following points should be observed.

- The assessment must represent the particular activities at all relevant locations, or the worst-case scenario should be assessed.

- There should not be any significant deviations from the assessment.

- The assumptions on which the assessment is based should be recorded, such as the safe working procedures detailed in the company health and safety policy statement that all work locations follow.

- The control measures that are in place should not deviate from that on which the assessment was based.

It would be advisable to ensure that more than one work location is assessed in order to balance out any discrepancies that might occur and an explanation of how the generic assessment was carried out would help to reassure all concerned.

There is no legal requirement for each activity at each work location to be assessed, just a requirement for the assessment to be 'suitable and sufficient'.

Persons who are particularly vulnerable

When carrying out risk assessments, consideration needs to be given to groups of people or individuals who may be, for various reasons, more susceptible to accidents or ill health in the workplace.

The following is a list of some groups who may be considered vulnerable. It is however, not exhaustive.

Vulnerable Groups	Reasons
Pregnant women and nursing mothers	Susceptible to variations of temperature, heavy weights, night or shift work, lead, hazardous substances, general fatigue, cramped working positions.
Visitors, contractors, members of the public	Would normally be unaware of dangers associated with the workplace and its layout therefore may disregard safety instructions.
Young persons	Immaturity can lead to carelessness and if they have had no previous industrial experience they may often be unaware of dangers.
People on work experience or government training schemes	Similar reasons as for young persons; also a willingness to please an employer may lead to their taking short-cuts.
Lone workers	Likely to be unable to summon help in an emergency and may also be susceptible to violence.
Temporary employees including those from employment agencies	Will be unaware of site and safety rules and may have less regard for the company and its equipment.
Disabled persons	Visual or hearing impairment may result in hazards not being noticed; physical impairment may make the operation of certain equipment difficult and access and egress from workstations and workplace may be a problem.
Employees with certain illnesses	Certain illnesses such as epilepsy may put people at increased risks from certain activities.
Peripatetic workers	No supervisor contact or monitoring, working methods not observed and varying work locations may contain risks.
Maintenance workers	Often work alone, sometimes with dangerous machinery. Possibility of machines being inadvertently switched on.

Special attention will therefore have to be paid to ensure that control measures introduced to control the risks to these vulnerable groups are sufficient.

Risk assessment checklist

A risk assessment should always be 'suitable and sufficient'. The following checklist outlines what should be included and is recommended for use when checking any risk assessment received from an employer:

- date risk assessment carried out

- job title

- description of job

- frequency of task

- hazards actual and potential

- consequences of the risk – low, medium or high

- non-routine jobs

- other staff affected

- workers particularly at risk – lone workers, people with disabilities, trainees etc.

- other people affected – the public, contractors etc.

- working environment

- legal standards that apply – Acts, Regulations etc.

- emergency procedures

- training

- monitoring – control measures and health surveillance

- recommended improvements (corrective actions)

- review date

- signature of competent person.

The HSE produce a guide to risk assessment called *Five Steps to Risk Assessment* (1999) for all employers. This a simple guide to completing an assessment of risk in the workplace. The five steps are:

1. Look for hazards.

2. Decide who might be harmed and how.

3. Evaluate the risks and decide whether the existing precautions are adequate or whether more should be done.

4.　Record your findings.

5.　Review your assessment and revise if necessary.

One final point for you to consider seriously is ensuring that you have a fully trained H & S officer in your organisation. It could be a job developer with a lead role in health and safety, but if you have a focus point for all the H & S information that is being generated and who can interpret its importance to you and your clients, you will be much better prepared for all eventualities.

You will be dealing with many different employers in many different industries and who have as many interpretations of what constitutes a health and safety policy. If you have the knowledge and experience, you will be able to identify work situations that may cause problems and have answers as to how to deal with them. The overwhelming majority of employers want to ensure that H & S regulations are followed, but fail to dedicate the resources to ensure that or review them on a regular basis. If you have that expertise then you will be offering a service that could enhance your reputation in the field.

JOB DEVELOPMENT PROSPECTS

Consider all training and career change opportunities.

- Will the person be able to change their job tasks?

- Can they work with larger or smaller groups of people?

- Will there be an opportunity for external and internal training programmes?

- In short, will they be able to develop in the job as they become more skilled and experienced?

JOB FLEXIBILITY

Will the employer consider changes that may be needed to accommodate unidentified needs?

Now complete Exercise 5.1.

Exercise 5.1

Consider all the elements of the job analysis form (starting with Company Details p.83) of your own job and gather all the information needed to have a clear picture of the details for each section.

- How long did it take?
- Did you know where to get all the information?
- Were there any surprises?
- Are there any aspects you would like to change?
- How can you start to make those changes?

Every employee is entitled to know all these details before they make a decision about taking a job.

JOB TASKS

Jobs are made up of many different routines and employees need to be able to fulfil the physical, intellectual and sensory requirements of the job to be successful. We therefore need to identify all the routines involved.

There are three basic categories of work routines:

- Main job tasks – the actual regularly repeated job tasks.

- Intermittent job tasks – associated with the main job tasks but which occur infrequently.

- Job-related tasks/routines – directly related to the job, vital to the performance, but sometimes not explicitly required, e.g. break times, use of protective clothing, shutting down machinery at break times.

These may change on a regular basis and there is a need to review the job tasks on a regular basis to ensure that the employee is being supported in appropriate ways. Similarly, it is important to note all the other requirements of the job – quality and speed needed or any physical abilities that are necessary.

OTHER WORKPLACE INFORMATION

There will be many areas to consider in this section – some may be unwritten rules, which are just as important for the person to understand as formal rules if they are to successfully integrate into the workplace culture. See Case Study 5.5.

Case Study 5.5

Bill, who has some moderate lerning difficulties, got a job in a factory where his liberal use of bad language would not be noticeable, as the work culture made this acceptable. What no-one had told Bill was that this liberalism didn't extend to the Managing Director, who was told to '**** off' by Bill when asked to move a few boxes in the gangway. Luckily, the MD saw the funny side of this and when the difference was explained to Bill, he understood and never made the same mistake.

EQUIPMENT AND MATERIALS USED

- Who supplies them to the workers?
- Who maintains them?
- Where are they kept?
- What are the rules for using them?
- What training is received?

INDEPENDENCE REQUIRED

- Is the person on his or her own all day?
- Is the person expected to get his or her own materials?
- Does he or she have to use initiative to complete job tasks?
- When a job is finished, does the person have to start the next job on his or her own?

SUPERVISION AVAILABLE

- Are there periods of direct supervision?
- Who does the supervising?

- Does the supervisor understand his or her role in relation to your client?

- Have you discussed the situation with the supervisor?

CO-WORKER CONTACT

- Are there co-workers in regular contact at the workstation?

- Is it a small team working together?

- Is it just a small/large group of workers completing tasks independently?

- Do they take breaks together?

- Do they have staff meetings?

OTHER CONSIDERATIONS

- When particular jobs come in, are there specific ways of working?

- Is this clear and explained unambiguously?

- Are there special tools for particular jobs?

- Does every piece of work have to pass stringent quality tests?

- Does the finished product need to be boxed, or presented or sent to the next department by a certain time?

Just keep an open mind about the workplace rules and regulations and try to get beneath the surface of the day-to-day job tasks to the real environmental conditions, so that you and your client are able to prepare for any potential concerns and have thought about ways in which changes can be made to bridge any gaps. If you can start on a positive note then you are well on the way to building a positive relationship with people, such as co-workers and supervisors, who can have a great impact on your client's success or failure in the job.

Now complete Exercise 5.2.

Exercise 5.2

Break down your own job into the three categories. Be sure to ask a colleague for their confirmation that you have noted down all the tasks and peripheral routines that you undertake.

- Is it more than you thought?
- Are there any surprises?

PHYSICAL ABILITY NEEDED

This is the physical ability as required by the job, not the person's abilities.

- Are there certain abilities that are essential?
- Is there potential for changes to be made in particular areas?

ACCOMMODATIONS/CHANGES

Changes can be made in a variety of ways: changing the working pattern, or environment; making adaptations to machinery; varying or changing the pattern of tasks etc. These are just some of the ways to help both employee and employer develop a sound, long-term working relationship.

You may want to consider discussing potential adaptations with the Employment Service's Disability Service Team (DST), usually accessed via the Disability Employment Adviser (DEA) based at the local job centre. They will have the knowledge of specialist aids and assessment of appropriate equipment that could make a positive difference to a client's chance of getting the job. They also have a package of financial aid that can make a substantial difference to the cost to an employer of providing aids and adaptations.

However, this is still another area in which the needs of the employee and the employer could come into conflict. If we have to make changes to support the employee what effect, if any, will this have on the employer?

Establishing an open and trusting relationship in the initial stages will help if changes need to be implemented. It is important to make sure that the changes are kept to the minimum necessary in order to achieve the goal of enabling the employee to be fully included in the workplace. It is also important to ensure that the client will make changes and compromise where appropriate so that the employer can see that the matching process is reciprocal.

The best support is the minimum amount necessary to ensure that the new employee becomes a valued member of the workforce. You then have to accept that the minimum amount of external 'interference' is also preferable (and that includes you!) We need to examine how we decide on the level of support.

This will need to be carefully monitored to ensure that we are not supporting in a way that is at odds with the natural support, or if it is necessary to change the support mechanism from the one normally used in that particular environment, that we keep all people fully informed and try to get agreement.

Natural work supports, that is, co-workers in the working environment, must be the starting point for filling support needs, irrespective of the level of severity of the client's disability or the gaps in the job match. The availability of a natural support should be established at the outset, to access the most effective way of learning the job. Someone who is familiar with the working environment – the dos and don'ts, the formal and informal rules, the social relationships that help the place tick over.

If these natural supports are appropriate and can be trained to support the potential employee, then more intrusive supports, e.g. job coaches/supporters need not be considered. If, however, it is felt that the support can only be adequately provided by a job coach or supporter then some basic questions need to be considered:

- When is it appropriate for a job coach to provide assistance?

- What type of assistance should be provided?

- What level of assistance is appropriate?

If we start by identifying the needs of the jobseeker, then it is important to realise that too much support is just as much a negative condition as inappropriate or too little support. If we have as our goal the eventual complete independence of the jobseeker in a positive employment situation, then we need to examine very carefully the level of support necessary to achieve that goal. The minimum support necessary offered for a successful conclusion will mean that the fading process will be all the more easy to achieve than if unnecessary support has been put in place. Once provided, that support is difficult to withdraw.

If you have no access to job coaches, it may well be advisable to map out the local support that is available. You may have to develop links with other local service providers with the relevant expertise in the area. Preparation of this nature will help you be confident of being able to deliver appropriate support quickly and effectively, giving both client and employer confidence in your professional approach to job development.

SUPERVISOR OR NATURAL SUPPORT EXPECTATIONS

The manager may have covered the broad-brush details of the job tasks, but the direct supervisor and co-workers may well have more detailed requirements that don't necessarily conflict with the management perspective but mean that there are other important considerations to be taken into account by new workers. It is best to discuss this with the direct supervisor and natural support and gain a picture of the real working environment. Spend some time going through the process with the people in the department, ensuring that the client gets to spend some time with them.

Now complete Exercise 5.3.

Exercise 5.3

Make a list of all your potential partners in the local area who could help in delivering your employment service.

- Do you already have a contact with them?
- Are there any potential partners who already have job coaches / job supporters?
- What have you and your service to offer potential partners?

EMPLOYER JOB CHARACTERISTICS/REQUIREMENTS

As previously discussed, this helps identify the main characteristics of the job and the skills needed to undertake it successfully. Looked at with the matching preferences/skills grid in the vocational profile it gives us a quick reference guide to the suitability of the job match. Check the grids against each other to see how close a match there is and whether any gaps in support can be identified.

This is, of course, looked at alongside the other information that has been gathered. It is important to note that individual factors may not be critical but once all criteria are covered, the results can be discussed with both the client and employer to see whether the analysis of the results is agreed. This should help identify any gaps in the support available and in the client's skills.

You may be able to deal with most gaps quickly; for example, an employee has some mobility problems and is unable to collect the materials to complete his job tasks. The employer agrees to rearrange the workstation so that materials are easily available. Or the employer only offers 32 hours per week when the client wanted 35 hours per week. The employee agrees to accept the 32 hours.

However, you may identify gaps that are much more difficult to accommodate and more innovative changes may need to be considered. Can the job be 'carved' so the problem task is excluded from the range of tasks to complete? You may also identify gaps that cannot be bridged and neither the client nor the employer can help. This may be the time to consider whether the match is appropriate. Help the client and employer examine all the factors and consider any possible routes through the problems. This may be the time to cut your losses and start the job search again. The client and employer should make the final decision with you supporting them.

SUPPORT NEEDS CHECKLIST AND WORK-RELATED SKILLS

Unless the employer already knows the individual this section can only be completed on the first review, but it will give a summary of the support needed in a range of job-related skills. This will be a great help when reviewing progress and evaluating any concerns. The client has an identical checklist in the vocational profile that should also fit into the first review.

The information from these checklists will feed into the Support Review Chart, if completed, and you can identify whether there are any major differences between the two checklists – is the client being realistic or is the employer being honest?

You may need to consider the situation if the two checklists are very similar – is this an overly positive view by both parties that will not stand up to scrutiny when it comes to moving to unsupported employment? Keep working on all aspects of the job and try to get an accurate picture of the real progress being made.

INFORMATION ANALYSIS

As with the vocational profile, complete a summary of all the relevant information collated for the job analysis. On the basis of this information you will be advising the potential employer and employee about the closeness of the job match, any gaps in support that will need to be addressed and any possible changes needed to achieve a successful job match.

Action points developed from the job analysis

EFFECTIVE SUPPORT

You need to develop effective support to suit individual needs and this will mean looking at the particular circumstance to see where on the support continuum the employee is located. This will depend on, amongst other aspects:

- the person being supported

- the nature and type of disability

- the complexity of what is to be learned

- the availability of feasible natural supports in the workplace.

Some guidelines are therefore needed to help you decide where to pitch the support level. For instance, identifying the gaps between the employee's skills and the needs of the job is vital. There are three main areas we need to examine: the information gap, the physical gap and the natural supports gap.

The information gap

This is caused by the problems that arise due to the way that job task information or instructions are presented and communicated in the workplace. The information may be given in such a way that it is not understood or is not remembered.

To overcome any initial skills gap it is generally possible to bring previous knowledge to new situations and an awareness of the many strategies to help us overcome the problem, e.g. trial and error, reading instructions, or asking someone who knows. However, it may be that the client's experience of work is limited and he or she does not have that previous knowledge. See Case Study 5.6.

Case Study 5.6

Bernard has short-term memory loss due to a road traffic accident, but has a real aptitude for managing a machine parts stores department. Previously, instructions to requisition parts were given over the telephone or verbally. This wasn't a problem if there were only one or two items but any more and Bernard found it difficult to remember all of them and consequently things were not sent to the workshop or the wrong part was sent. A computer link has now been installed so that Bernard can see the list and work to that. He also has a small tape recorder that he can play back to make sure he gets the requisition right.

The physical gap

This can arise when the layout of the workplace is unsuitable for the client. For example, it could be that access into the building is not possible, there are no accessible toilet facilities, or the workbenches are too high or low.

This can be the easiest of the gaps to bridge if you can get the employer committed to the process, as there is an Access to Work programme via the Employment Service that can fund a large proportion of the costs of any aids and adaptations to premises that help accommodate people with disabilities. Also, employers can see the difference that physical changes can make whereas the other gaps can be more problematic.

The natural supports gap

This refers to problems that arise due to the absence of natural supports and it occurs when there are no suitable co-workers available to help the new employee gain the necessary skills and knowledge to succeed in the job tasks required by the employer.

The type and seriousness of the gap naturally affect the method of appropriate support chosen in order to bridge that gap. See Case Study 5.7.

Case Study 5.7

Julia had previously worked in a clerical capacity before developing a mental health problem. Having achieved a stable recovery, she looked for a job in which she could recover some of her previous skills. She felt a small office may be best and a job was found that suited her perceived needs – working in the office of a landscape gardener. Her employer knew all aspects of the work and was willing to train Julia to undertake the admin duties. Unfortunately, it transpired that he was increasingly drawn into the fieldwork, leaving Julia to cope with the admin with only a bare minimum of training. Consequently, there were some mistakes made which he felt should have been spotted and it ended with Julia leaving, feeling very undervalued. Fortunately, she is now in employment in a large office, but one where she can get the day-to-day support she needs in the initial stages of her return to work.

ESTABLISHING OR IMPROVING RELATIONSHIPS BETWEEN EMPLOYEE AND EMPLOYER

Whatever the initial support needs, establishing relationships between employers and jobseekers/employees is an important goal of supported employment services and leads to unsupported employment being considered.

This goal defines your role in the supported employment process. It is that of a catalyst, bringing both partners together into a long-term sustainable relationship. This also has direct implications for the level of support offered – you not only need to offer the minimum level of effective support but also to use the in-house support mechanisms wherever possible. See Case Study 5.8.

Case Study 5.8

Francis has had a profound hearing impairment since birth, and has little speech. He can use basic British Sign Language (BSL) but is reluctant to do so and prefers not to communicate with anyone but his family. With the support of a social worker for the deaf to interpret at the meetings with the job developer, a profile of Francis' needs and aspirations began to be established. He did not, under any circumstances, want an interpreter to work with him in any job and just wanted to get on with it. The job developer found a potential job in the local Priory residential school, working with the head gardener producing vegetables and fruit and keeping the extensive grounds in order. The attitude of the head gardener was going to be crucial if this job was to be developed, as Francis found it difficult to establish relationships and had been known to be aggressive when frustrated. The head gardener worked with Francis on a job taster for three days going through the variety of jobs and offering Francis the opportunity to try the jobs out. They hardly communicated except through gesticulation and demonstration of the work. Francis showed a good aptitude for picking up the work from the step-by-step demonstration that was given by the head gardener in a calm and patient way. Their relationship began to develop into a strong bond of trust and they constructed their own communication system to such an extent that when the job developer visited, Francis no longer wanted the interpreter there and relied on the head gardener to translate. Francis became much more confident outside work as well and most of his aggressive behaviour disappeared. The extra time the head gardener spent with Francis meant that some tasks had to be completed by other co-workers and the funding supported this until it was no longer needed.

Clear careful planning is needed to avoid 'breakdown calls'. The goal to achieve is that of giving the employee the chance of becoming a contributing and valued member of the workforce.

- The quicker we are able to help build a positive working relationship between the employee and his or her co-workers and employer, the sooner this goal will be achieved.

- We need to be on the periphery.

- We should be considered a resource not a dependency.

Involving the co-workers in the task analysis and job-matching process recognises the contribution they can make and paves the way for the establishment of a positive relationship. Then you need to ensure, if necessary, that the co-worker is involved from the time the employee starts work, with the support worker advising from the background. The co-worker will have direct knowledge and experience of the working environment – 'Yes, we do it that way, but there are these other options that work just as well.'

JOB MATCHING

Introduction

As noted, once completed the vocational profile and job analysis need to be jointly assessed to ensure that all support needs are identified and strategies for meeting those needs are made. If the match is viable then part two of the Development Plan (see Appendix 4) should be completed, detailing all actions needed to achieve progression. If, however, the gaps are insurmountable, then the match will not be viable and job finding will have to restart. (See Appendix 8 for a copy of the job-matching form.)

Job-matching process

The process of job matching at its most basic level is that of comparing the information from the client's vocational profile with the characteristics of an available job, as outlined in the job analysis, and then detailing the way in which you will try to bridge the gaps between the two. Obviously, the employer and employee have the major part to play in this process.

There will be times when a 'perfect' match is found but other issues prevent it being progressed. Learn and move on. See Case Study 5.9.

Case Study 5.9

James, a 28-year-old with cerebral palsy, had never worked. He approached a supported employment service expressing the desire to work in a field related to supporting people with disabilities in recreational activities. With the support of a job-finding and support agency, two potentially suitable matches were found: one in a new recreational service specialising in supporting people with learning disabilities and physical disabilities to access sports and leisure facilities; the other at a local sports stadium where they were looking to involve people with disabilities in using the leisure facilities. James' vocational profile seemed to match almost perfectly with both opportunities, but after a job-taster visit to the recreational service he didn't turn up for the second visit and would not follow up requests for visits. Finally, he said that he didn't want to go through with the jobs as he felt that he couldn't put himself under the pressure of possibly failing at the job and the effect this would have on his benefits. What the agency hadn't done is to take into account the many years James had never been in employment and the effect this had on his self-esteem and the reliance he had on the benefits system. He appeared to be a confident and friendly person and the agency felt he could go into work straight away, without any confidence-building support or clear understanding about the impact of earning a wage on his benefits. A slightly different approach, with James developing skills alongside someone else, without a direct move into employment and a clear picture of the effect on benefits, could have made a difference.

Establishing supported employment places in the workplace attempts to bring together many different organisational and individual preferences and needs. Not only do you need to work out your approach very carefully, you also need to be clear about what the relationship is between you and the person with a disability and the employer; both are customers consuming your services.

This reflects a significant change in how support services view people with disabilities and employers. Rather than being people who need treatment or care, those with disabilities are seen as empowered individuals with individual choice, making decisions about future direction and routes to achieve their goals. Employers are not charity sponsors, they are customers and business partners, and your service is helping them to recruit new staff and make the necessary changes to ensure a successful working relationship with a new employee.

You must identify the needs of the employers and offer services to meet those needs in the same way that you identify and meet the needs of people with disabilities. In establishing a working relationship with both of your customers you have to look to the long-term success of the employee in work.

Now complete Exercise 5.4.

Exercise 5.4

Imagine that you are an employer in your local area and a supported employment service contacts you with a proposal to develop a job for a person with a disability.

- What are the most important things you would expect from that service?
- What would you want to know about the person involved?
- What would you expect the service to know about your business?

Now put yourself back in the position of being a service provider.

- How would you look to get that information?
- Moreover, would it all be appropriate?

Finally it would be worthwhile to mention the possible use of the task analysis (TA) in using co-worker support and closing the support needs gap. Systematic instruction (SI) is a highly specialised support skill and should be undertaken by a suitably trained job coach.

It will not be appropriate to discuss SI in any detail here, but if there is a need for such support, then ensure that you have access to a qualified trainer. However, a brief discussion of the task-analysis process, breaking down tasks into manageable steps, might be useful.

TASK ANALYSIS

People with disabilities have the same abilities to master complex tasks if the training and support is effective and carried out appropriately. Task analysis is a method of breaking down a job task into a step-by-step process, following the natural course of the task as closely as possible. It is done in order to support the training of an individual more effectively by pinpointing the specific steps that are causing problems.

The job developer first works with the co-worker who has expertise in the task (and may be the natural job support) to get a clear understanding of the task in order to help with the training. It may be that the client is able to follow the normal training routine, or the task may have to be broken down into steps and each step taught in sequence.

Having identified the gap (see pages 107–108) a decision needs to be made as to what assistance and type of support is appropriate. Assistance may take a variety of forms, for example, verbal instructions, 'sitting with Nellie', non-verbal communication, gestures, physical guidance, sign language, written instructions or pictures for people who cannot read. What you need to do is determine the client's most effective learning style.

It could also take the form of adaptations such as access ramps, handrails or other facilities, technical assistance usually associated with tasks on the job, or rearranging a workstation or equipment to make the task more accessible. It is vital that the type of assistance is appropriate to the individual's needs in completing the job task, otherwise his or her progress will be delayed – and the reaction of co-workers can be critical.

To reiterate, the job developer should advise upon the most appropriate level of assistance and type of support, always looking towards the lowest possible level of 'interference' needed to give the most effective support.

This method of training will not prevent all mistakes and whilst you may be able to anticipate most it is right to allow the individual to take risks and develop within a learning environment. People should be allowed to find their own way through unless it gets to the point where they are continually frustrated and cannot complete the task without mistakes. A way around this which still achieves the goal of minimum interference, would be to develop a way in which the individual could review his or her own work and self-correct. For example, if a completed item was on view then the individual could check the item being worked on against this for errors.

Clearly it is important to find out before the task analysis is attempted whether the person is having difficulties with the job tasks. The Certificate in Supported Employment distance learning course uses the everyday example of making a cup of tea. The first step could well be to plug in the kettle and switch it on. However, this may be a big step for an individual and could be broken down even further to:

place hand on plug
pick up plug
locate pins in socket
push plug home
switch on power.

(Foundation Programme in Supported Employment 2000, p.76)

This could mean the need for a more intensive support process, for instance, systematic instruction (SI), which is based on a behaviourist approach using stimuli response in the working environment. The examination of this approach is beyond the scope of this workbook.

The vocational profile and job analysis should have helped identify any gaps that could adversely affect the person's ability to complete the tasks efficiently. The extent to which the task analysis is applicable will depend on each person's particular support requirements. The level of detail will vary from simply identifying aspects of the tasks of a job, through observing the job being done, to undertaking the task oneself and carefully recording each step in detail.

When we perform a task this chain of steps is usually an unconscious process. However, the reason for breaking down the chain is precisely because the individuals we support may be unable to perform the tasks in this unconscious way. The aim of the task analysis is to aid learning and instil in the individual the links between steps until the task can be dealt with in much the same way as it would be in a regular situation.

The task analysis, then, is developed so that the trainer understands the task to be learnt by the trainee and tailors the training method as closely as possible to the needs of the individual. Of course, the trainer should know the work routines thoroughly before attempting to support an individual in learning those tasks. This is why close co-operation with co-workers and supervisors is essential and the training should be completed by the natural support wherever possible.

It can be an intensive and very intrusive process and should be used with great care. Fading out such support should be completed as quickly as possible. Consider undertaking specific training prior to undertaking this form of support.

Now complete Exercise 5.5.

Exercise 5.5

Consider the task of making a cup of tea or a task in your work and break it down into the different steps that make up the whole task so that you could teach them in an organised way to someone who had no knowledge of the job. Get a colleague to be 'lab rat' and go through the steps of the task using demonstration and reading the steps out so your colleague can undertake the task.

- Did the 'simple' job break down into a few steps?
- Did you read or demonstrate the task and did it lead to success?
- If you were given the list of different steps, could you construct the task?
- Would the list of steps be more useful than a demonstration?
- Is a demonstration more 'interference' than verbal instruction would be?

Chapter 6

Support Review Process

Introduction

The vocational profile is completed, development plan implemented, job found, employment negotiated, job analysis carried out and matching process begun and the client is in work. Can you sit back on your laurels? No, of course not. You need to ensure that the job opportunity is on course to achieve its aim; sustained employment whether with continuing long-term support or into unsupported employment.

You have completed all the above processes and the employee is now some way into the job; possibly three months or six months, depending on individual circumstances and agreed review process.

The next part of the process is the support review, which involves examining all the elements that have gone before and evaluating, with the client and the employer, whether there are any changing support needs and how the job match is holding up. This is where the principle of the vocational profile and job analysis being 'live' documents is evident. Also, remember your role as the catalyst, ensuring that the working relationship between the client and employer is at the forefront of your development strategy.

The support review process is made up of several parts starting with the Ongoing Support Review (OSR) that can lead to the Support Review Chart (SRC) and then onto the Overall Job Review (OJR) when we are closer to the goal of unsupported employment.

Ongoing Support Review (OSR)

If you are at this stage in the support process for a client you will have, in the previous two to four weeks, completed a vocational profile and job analysis review focusing on the individual skills and preferences and the job characteristics and skills and any information gathered over the previous few months on issues relating to the employment situation.

The first meeting with the employee and employer in this process will consider all ongoing support needs and any movement in the job match elements. You will agree

- a change in support if there has been a deterioration, or

- continuance of support, if there has been a steady improvement, or

- fading of support, if improvement is at a level that support is no longer required.

Use part three of the development plan (See Appendix 4) to summarise the review discussion and any new actions agreed in order to enhance the development process.

You may well find that your original plan is working well and both employee and employer are developing a positive relationship that will, if everything continues on its present course, lead to unsupported employment.

However, you may find that one, some or all the elements of the job are a concern for either or both the employee and employer, paying particular attention to the vocational profile / job analysis support review pages. In this case, the Ongoing Support Review may resolve these issues and get you back on course. Always ensure that both employee and employer agree and give their signatures to all aspects of the development plan.

If the Ongoing Support Review does not resolve these issues then you may have to use other ways of identifying underlying issues or persuading the employee and employer that they are going to have to acknowledge the development process is different from their perceptions of it.

This can be a difficult, time-consuming and stressful process and you will have to brace yourself for the potential confrontations with either client or employer or both! The client may be fearful that fading support from you will leave him or her isolated in the frightening world of self-determination and independence, or the employer may have become complacent with a status quo in which you have been responsible for the support issues, or have become reliant on the funding that you are about to take away.

You will need to measure each situation and make decisions, offering advice and support, which will lead to a successful conclusion for the client and the employer. See Case Study 6.1.

Case Study 6.1

Paul, working in an inner city supermarket, was an excellent shelf stacker with detailed product knowledge and he enjoyed helping customers around the store. However, he found remembering lists of instructions for a full shift too difficult and gravitated towards tasks he liked rather than those he had been instructed to complete. Paul's line manager found this frustrating and irritating but, following advice from the job developer, instructions were given at shorter intervals and supervision made more regularly, which made a very positive difference not only to Paul's performance but to the line manager's stress levels! The line manager on reflection began to see that the frustrations he had been feeling were a result of his own inexperience with people with disabilities and the practical and moral support offered by the job developer made a very big difference. He also began to realise that all employees had a range of different needs and if he could try to accommodate them without affecting the efficiency of the store then it would lead to a much happier and more effective workforce.

The Support Review Chart (SRC)

This is a potentially useful tool in helping you resolve any issues around progress when employee and employer do not agree on either the present position or future development. For a copy of the Support Review Chart, see Appendix 9a; Appendix 9b is a completed example.

The aim of the Support Review Chart is to monitor and facilitate the training and development of people with disabilities in supported employment. It attempts to pinpoint best practice and achievements as well as areas that need support.

The starting point for this approach is to ensure that both the employee and employer understand the need for development and then to focus on the specific 'gaps', actual or perceived, that have to be closed to facilitate that development.

Both the employee and employer will, hopefully, make a positive contribution to the review, facilitated by your job developer, and will give the monitoring meetings a firm, practical base from which to work. The review will also ensure that the employer/supervisor has a clear view, based on actual examples, of the individual's development and that the relationship is clearly aiming for progression.

The Support Review Chart will help develop the relationship between the employee and employer by ensuring that progression in a range of job-related skills is formally noted and any weaknesses (on either side) are strengthened through inclusion in the Ongoing Support Review. It will allow all parties to the plan to identify what stage they are at in progressing through supported employment towards the potential goal of open employment.

It will also help you to evaluate how effective your service is in attaining the service aims and objectives based around inclusion and self-determination.

This Support Review Chart will supplement and strengthen employer action plans/appraisals that are usually about a year-on-year job task improvement whereas the Ongoing Support Review focuses upon individual progression to open employment and takes a longer-term view.

Process

The first stage, as already noted, will be to undertake the Ongoing Support Review. If issues cannot be resolved, you could consider getting the employee and employer to complete the chart. This consists of four main areas:

- Job Tasks
- Communication
- Training
- Reliability

For example, communication is about a variety of skills: working well with others, building social relationships, appropriate behaviours, showing respect for co-workers, as well as specific communication issues, e.g. speech and gesture. If a client completes this section, putting a cross in box 5, and offers examples such as 'always polite', 'talks to co-workers at break times', 'understands that as part of a team he has certain responsibilities to support the team effort' you can get a clear picture of how he feels the situation is progressing. If, however, the employer puts a cross in box 2 and offers examples such as 'never talks to co-workers', 'is always making comments about others and won't try to work as a team member', then the two views conflict with each other and this is a major cause for concern.

It may well be that the employer, or supervisor, has an entirely wrong picture of the real situation. What is important is that you investigate and find out the real picture and try to get both parties to agree before you can address any issues. The examples are vital as this will be the basis of your discussion.

Whilst the initial completion of the chart is quantitive, the main input for this review will be in the examples of performance given by both the employer and employee. This will enable you to examine current practice and whether or not there is consensus between the parties as to how well the person is being supported.

It will also enable you to look at any inaccurate views of the work situation held either by the employer or employee. It will mean they have to justify any perceptions with concrete examples and possibly have that challenged by the other partner. This is essential if you are to both get an accurate picture of the employment situation and any areas that need to be worked on in order to progress the person, either within supported employment or into open employment. See Case Study 6.2.

Case Study 6.2

Jane worked in a large factory that had a self-use staff canteen, complete with fridge, cooker and storage facilities. An Ongoing Support Review was undertaken and the supervisor identified a couple of areas of concern that didn't match up to co-workers' reports on performance. The job developer felt that a Support Review Chart might help and both the employee and employer completed the chart and a meeting was arranged to discuss the results. The major area of concern was Jane's behaviour, which the supervisor had identified as inappropriate, based around one incident in the staff canteen. She opened the fridge, taking drinks out for her co-workers and shutting the fridge door rather heavily with her foot and using the same method to open the canteen door, almost in the face of the supervisor.

Jane was able to answer this directly by saying that she was only following the same practice as her work-mates, as it wasn't possible to carry the drinks in one go (there being a company rule about one journey only for the drinks break) without using her feet to open doors. The supervisor checked this out and it was backed up by her co-workers. The rule was changed and so was the

Case Study 6.2 continued

> attitude of the supervisor who had based her negative report on this one incident. The following review was seen to include information from co-workers as well, which finally persuaded the employer to support the view that open employment was a realistic option for the year-end. Jane is now in open employment.

Now complete Exercise 6.1.

Exercise 6.1

Consider the results from the completed charts in the first two sheets of Appendix 9b. (Don't look yet at the completed third sheet that has the details of the actual meeting on it.)

- What are the major differences?
- What are the implications of these differences for progression?
- What should a meeting between employee and employer, following completion of the charts, concentrate on?
- Can you suggest any strategies that might have a positive effect on these differences?
- Now look at the completed meeting sheet and see whether your discussion is similar to the one carried out.
- What objectives would you set for the development plan based on the information from this meeting?

As stated, the views of the client and employer provide the essential input into the support review. The job developer will play a facilitating role. Each party will make an assessment of performance within the four key categories: job task skills, communication skills, training and reliability. More specific performance criteria comprise these categories. These can be referred to in helping to make category assessments. For example, the criterion 'meets required work standard' falls under the 'Job Tasks' category.

Although the criteria within each category are broad, this is an advantage because it will cover a range of jobs and allow both employee and employer to illustrate their positions with specific and relevant examples of the current position.

When making an assessment, participants will assign a score for each category. The scale is from 1 to 5, with 1 being 'never' and 5 being 'always'. Lower points on the scale would indicate a less favourable position (1, 2) and higher points (4, 5) a more favourable position; 3 would be average. The use of specific examples to support the assessment is vital and will help prevent participants giving arbitrary scores on the review. It will also help to identify areas for improvement in work performance and items to include in the support review. See Case Study 6.3.

Case Study 6.3

Joe was having some difficulty at work and the employer felt he wasn't putting in the same effort that he used to. After completion of the Support Review Chart the major area of contention related to the need for training after the installation of new machinery. Both parties felt that training was a problem with the employer saying it was because Joe had not wanted to train. The job developer pursued this issue and after some investigation it transpired that the supervisor, trying to protect Joe, had not put him forward for the training as he felt it would be too difficult for him. This had caused Joe difficulties as he was still expected to work in the new ways resulting from the job task changes. The employer arranged more training and included Joe. It was difficult for Joe and he did need more support in the initial stages but has progressed quite well and the employer is now quite happy with the results and Joe is pleased, as he feels he has successfully learnt new skills and is contributing more effectively. What had been a general misgiving about overall performance became a specific issue that was resolved fairly easily.

Total scores within each category are added together to form an overall development score. Eventually, after the first review, progress can be compared with past scores to gauge how well the development strategy is progressing.

Ensure that a job task list is attached to each Support Review Chart and any changes are identified during the next review process. The potential for development by trying out other job tasks could also be discussed with the client.

When completing the Support Review Chart during a review visit, examples of each criterion are listed on the form to help you, the client and employer consider appropriate examples that illustrate the particular viewpoint.

To reiterate, the Support Review Chart is based upon an evaluation of the client's progress in job-related skill areas. It is, initially, a quantitive evaluation but using qualitative examples to support the evaluation. Its purpose is to strengthen the relationship between the employer and employee by bringing them together to agree what progress is being made and what needs to be done in the future to sustain that development. It may identify a need for change in either the employer or employee and should be used, primarily, as a development tool not as a way to apportion blame for either lack of progress or lack of support.

Does it work?

A small pilot study has been carried out using the Support Review Chart and the findings so far suggest that both employees and employers make a positive contribution and are able to offer specific examples of progress or development issues. It has also helped clear up misunderstandings and inaccurate impressions of individual performance.

An interesting but perhaps unsurprising result to date has been that, in the overall scores given by each of the participants, employees are more positive about their skill levels than their employers. This sort of result may well have been anticipated but it is useful to have it identified. If either party has unrealistic or inaccurate perceptions about progress then it will help to gain a more accurate picture of real performance based on real examples. This can also lead to developing better strategies for progression and supporting development needs in the future.

The author is currently evaluating the Support Review Chart and would welcome any data collated in the course of using this tool. The data would, of course, remain strictly confidential. If you are interested in taking part in this evaluation the Support Review Chart is available as a spreadsheet application for ease of data collection and analysis. You can contact the author via the contact information at the back of this workbook.

An important point to make here is that in supporting people with learning difficulties to complete the chart you will need to make clear your explanation about the different elements and try to relate the scoring system to areas of their life or work that they can understand. Having completed the Support Review Chart with some people with learning difficulties, it has proved to be very useful and they have been able to relate specific examples in all areas that supported the view that they understood the process and that progression was important.

A meeting, post evaluation, should be arranged in order to discuss the results with both employee and employer and to find ways of addressing any needs that have been identified from the examples. These details should be added to part three of the Development Plan (see Appendix 4) and signed by all parties.

There has been some concern expressed, by some job developers during the pilot, about the Support Review Process in general and the Support Review Chart in particular, suggesting that it devalues the employer's appraisal system, excludes the individual and creates an artificial situation measuring skills; no other employee in the company has such a support review. Well, perhaps they should!

You will have to accept that this is a unique employment situation and your supported employment service has a clear remit to ensure that the client is supported as effectively as possible to progress towards open employment – a goal, sometimes conveniently forgotten, that all other employees in the company have already achieved.

Whilst you have to ensure that a positive relationship is developed independently between the client and the employer you can use your expertise, experience, funding, advice and support to help achieve this. Preparing a specific development plan and reviewing progression on an ongoing basis is not discriminatory. You are attempting to achieve a positive agreed goal for the client and this is clearly the foundation on which you should base your service.

The Support Review Chart will focus upon the development of the individual and link it to progression into open employment.

On-the-job support

During the support review process, you may be faced with a situation in which the individual has not undertaken the actual job tasks before and the job developer will need to ensure that the appropriate training and support are in place to keep the job match a viable one.

What we tend to forget is that we all started out at this point earlier in our working lives, with a need to train and get support in order to develop the skills to do our jobs effectively. If we showed aptitude, commitment and interest then the errors we inevitably made were accepted and dealt with and the learning process continued.

This is a perfectly acceptable process for any employer to be facing. Don't apologise or be diffident and don't expect to implement a perfect match in which the employee moves faultlessly into a sustainable employment situation.

People with disabilities are only asking for the same consideration with the training and support suited to their needs in order for them to develop the skills that will lead to sustainable employment. Look carefully for the point in the process where the employee and employer move from the perspective in which every problem is potentially disastrous and indicates that the match is not working to one in which the problems that arise are considered with the question, 'Now, how can we resolve this issue?' At this point, you will be well on the way to achieving success.

Ongoing support and fading

At the start there will probably be a period of high support needs, but as confidence builds and skills develop, the support should become more refined and should probably fade.

Remember: the minimum support necessary to achieve success. This is the time to begin to negotiate with the client and employer a continuing withdrawal of support. If the relationship has strengthened sufficiently between employer and employee this can be approached head on and a fading strategy can be decided quickly.

If there is still concern from either or both employer and employee, this negotiation will need to be more carefully considered. The Support Review Chart will be a very useful tool here, as it offers documented evidence and information over time about progression and fading support that has been endorsed by both employee and employer and will be hard to argue with.

A support bridge

It may well be that it is the thought of losing your personal support that is the issue. You will need to assure both employee and employer that your service will still be available for advice and support for some time following a successful transition into open employment.

There could be issues that you can help with that are not directly related to the job but which may affect the success of the transfer, i.e. housing problems, family conflict, co-worker conflict.

If you wish to see more people with disabilities in long-term, sustainable employment then you will have to commit to this extended support for some people. There are several considerable advantages for the service as well in accepting this responsibility.

- A successfully negotiated permanent job for the client.

- Continuing contact with a positive employer – a visible reference for your service and a potential future employer for other clients.

- A source of independent support for the client.

- Continued development of expertise in the support process.

Examples of Support Review Chart elements

JOB TASKS

- Meets required work standard – end product does not need to be re-made or re-provided because of earlier mistakes. For example, order picking: selecting the correct items and quantities for the customer at the first attempt within a reasonable timescale.

- Able to perform different tasks – finds no difficulty finishing one task and starting a different one. For example, administration: finishes filing documents and then collects outgoing post in the afternoon.

- Undertakes tasks independently – needs no assistance from others in performing tasks expected within the job. For example, driving: reads fuel gauge before starting a delivery and 'fills up' if there is not enough fuel in the tank.

- Able to use own initiative – responds effectively to situations where a prompt decision or action is needed. For example, catering: clearing used plates and cutlery from tables after customers have finished eating and left, in order to maintain sufficient seating capacity during busy periods.

COMMUNICATION

- Works well with others – able to interact with other people in order to successfully accomplish particular tasks. For example, administration: arranging with other staff to deal with telephone enquiries and provide general office cover during lunch breaks.

- Builds social relationships – participates in conversations, humour, team meetings and social functions. For example, going to the pub after work to share in the celebration of a colleague's examination result or promotion.

- Behaves appropriately – complies with behavioural expectations of employer, other staff and customers. For example, retail: helping customers, in a courteous manner, find items they are looking for by either directing them to the right place, or by taking them there personally.

- Shows respect for others – understands the needs and wishes of other people and acts respectfully towards them. For example, catering: listens and positively responds to criticism from customers about the taste of a dish that he or she has had the responsibility of preparing.

TRAINING

- Willing to undertake internal training – includes training delivered by staff within the host organisation, usually at the place of work. ('On-the-job' training, company courses such as time management and presentation skills.)

- Willing to undertake external training – includes training delivered or assessed by organisations other than the host, either at the place of work or at 'off-site' locations. (Industrial/professional training, NVQ qualifications, manual lifting, first aid at work.)

- Positively benefits from training experience – developments in work performance, knowledge, attitude or confidence, are noticeable having undertaken training.

RELIABILITY

- Can be trusted with company resources – can be trusted to look after company property or finances without the fear of abuse. For example, retail: demonstrating honesty about cash handling and giving the correct change.

- Demonstrates good attendance and punctuality – the client informs the company of his or her absence from work by following the set procedure for this. Absences from work are also supported by legitimate reasons and are not later discovered to be fabrications. For example, production: contacting the works supervisor at 8.00am before the start of the shift.

- Dresses appropriately for work – complies with dress code and observes the appropriate personal hygiene standards. For example, catering: always wearing clean aprons in the kitchen and restaurant areas and washing hands regularly before preparing and serving food.

Overall Job Review (OJR)

Introduction

The Overall Job Review (OJR) is an attempt to formalise actions that will help move employees closer to their career aspirations within their place of work and lead to achieving long-term, sustainable and unsupported employment. It brings together all the previous information, reviews and plans in order to focus on the progression to open employment. It provides a commitment towards maximising the employee's potential within his or her particular job, work environment and culture.

Process

The Overall Job Review will use the Ongoing Support Review and the vocational profile and job analysis reviews to continue the developmental process. Hence, both the employee and employer will jointly be responsible for developing the Overall Job Review and the employment officer will play a facilitating role. It documents the actions needed, based upon examples of work performance identified in the Ongoing Support Review.

For example, comments in the Ongoing Support Review may indicate that the employee is experiencing difficulty performing a particular task. See Case Study 6.4.

Case Study 6.4

'John does not return to remove empty boxes in the aisles after serving customers.'

'Serves customers begrudgingly, if he is in the middle of cleaning the shelves.'

The following action points may then be identified for inclusion on the Overall Job Review and the importance of customer care standards explained to John in a one-to-one setting:

Case Study 6.4 continued

- John only cleans the shelves when there is somebody else available to see to the customers.

- John visually checks the aisles for boxes after serving every customer.

- John sticks a price label onto his hand to remind him to return to his boxes after serving customers.

- John brings the recycling bin closer to his area of activity so there is less chance of boxes being left on the floor.

It is evident, then, that action points may not necessarily all be about changing the client. The answer could involve changing staffing levels, methods of working or the use of workplace aids. These should be documented in the Overall Job Review, but should also be recorded in other areas of the Development Plan, if appropriate.

Now complete Exercise 6.2.

Exercise 6.2

Consider the most appropriate type of support you would advise in the above example.
- Would it be natural support or a job coach or both?
- Would the support be different at different points in the plan?

Changes in the tasks that the employee is expected to perform must be recorded in an updated job analysis. Changes in the employee's abilities and support need levels must be recorded in an updated vocational profile. For example, altering working hours so that the employee starts work at a later time and securing 'Fares to work' through the Access to Work programme could represent two particular action points.

Recording these within the job analysis and vocational profile will help you to determine to what extent the employee's current job and the employee's perceptions of his or her ideal job have come together. As the 'match' gets increasingly close and work performance continues to improve, the prospect of open employment can become more of a reality for the client and company concerned.

The Overall Job Review should bring all elements together, providing an opportunity to make formal changes to either the job analysis or the vocational profile planning for fading support and achieving closure.

Many employers will have their own system of monitoring and appraising staff performance. Where does this fit in to our Overall Job Review? Feedback on the employee's efforts to achieve company performance objectives and factors that have been instrumental to their achievement/non-achievement will help the identification of action points within the Overall Job Review. Equally, action points identified within the Overall Job Review will inform the setting of company performance objectives for that individual. They may pick up on the need for smaller incremental developments before the achievement of a particular company performance objective.

Clearly then, our system is not intended to supersede that of the employer, but rather to work hand-in-hand with it. We have an obligation to prioritise individual development as well as to meet the requirements of the employer. That is why the development plan is important both for the client and the development of our service.

Conclusion

The Overall Job Review takes a broad look at the issue of client development. It retains a client focus whilst still acknowledging that there may be other factors that are needed to improve work performance. Therefore, the client's development becomes a shared responsibility rather than one that is simply devolved to the client. This has in the past allowed employers to disassociate themselves from the client when things do not proceed in the way the employer feels they should. We feel that ownership should be shared between the two principal parties in the employment relationship, the employee and the employer, and this is what the Overall Job Review aims to achieve.

The continuous nature of the process will facilitate the client's gradual transition from supported employment to open employment, providing the necessary support and changes along the way.

Chapter 7

Progression to Unsupported Employment

Introduction

Unsupported Employment: The Final Frontier – now is the time to find out whether the support strategy you have helped to develop since the initial contact has actually worked.

Whilst it is true that this goal may not be on the agenda for a significant number of people using supported employment services and a continuing contribution with significant levels of support will be the only possible outcome for some, it is right that we finish on this note. It may be that the person supported through your service, with the help of job supporters, the occupational therapist and social workers, will never achieve unsupported employment.

If we have unsupported employment as a potential goal for everyone, we are truly ensuring that we support the maximum progression towards independence that personal circumstances will allow at a particular point in time. All services should have the principles of supported employment as the cornerstone of their support and the attainment of maximum progression for the individual as the service goal.

Consider whether:

- the relationship between the employee and employer is strong enough for a move to unsupported employment to be agreed

- the client feel positive about his or her contribution in the workplace

- there is a natural support who is willing to continue that support

- the employer knows that you will still be available for advice following the move.

These matters and many more need to be considered. The Supported Employment Development Initiative (SEDI) projects identified some good practice to help achieve this closure. Do you use any of them?

Examples of Good Practice Identified within the SEDI Projects

- For employment to succeed the employer has to be impressed by the employee – able to make a positive contribution and appreciate what is important to the employer.

- Find consensus as to what is achievable and realistic and whether the employee can move to unsupported employment.

- Raise disability awareness as an issue with the employer before negotiating a place – raising awareness within the workforce and starting to form an informal network of support.

- Market the service as a 'facility' to both employee and employer.

- Work hard in partnership with the employer – assessing their commitment and sharing the belief in progression.

- Assess objections and obstacles realistically and honestly.

- Develop a library of information resources within your service.

- Ensure that you have the minimum information necessary to enable an effective job-matching process – a comprehensive vocational profile and job analysis.

- Assess client expectations of work and identify whether their job search is a realistic option, as this helps direct limited resources.

- Ensure that the employer and employee are aware of the full range of your support resources to help achieve progression.

- Ensure the natural support is someone:

> - in regular contact with the new employee
>
> - willing and capable of supporting the new employee
>
> - capable of advocating on the part of the new employee
>
> - patient, with an understanding of disability issues and able to see when the need to withdraw is necessary
>
> - Ensure that your staff are trained in the principles of supported employment and the concept of full inclusion.

These are just some of the examples of good practice advocated by SEDI projects nationally.

Process

Progression to unsupported employment will not usually mean that the employee/employer relationship has taken the same course as other employees or that it will ever be the same. What it should mean, however, is that both are satisfied that their needs are being met and the right support is in place for that to continue. Even if the right support still has to be used the employer is confident that they can still commit to providing that support without using your service; both mutually benefit from the continuing relationship to the degree that unsupported employment is appropriate.

> ## Employers' comments on supporting people into unsupported employment
>
> 'John works hard. He still needs some support but we feel it is important to acknowledge the work he does.'
>
> 'We are a local employer and it is important to put something back into the community. Jane is always on time, she is always helpful, she always does her best, we should do ours.'

These comments from employers on supporting people into unsupported employment are about their commitment to the individual they have come to value as a contributor to their company. This is why the emphasis on developing the employee/employer relationship cannot be too great. It is vital:

- to offer the minimum support necessary

- to fade your support out sooner rather than later

- to find and plug the gaps in the job match

- to work with co-workers on building relationships so they will also feel positive about working creatively to support the continuing employment of the individual.

You are probably never going to mould the person into becoming the average employee and should never try, but you will need to help make the most powerful argument possible to ensure that the individual is seen as an integral part of the regular workforce, with co-workers and employer working towards making the endeavour a success.

You are also helping the employee to commit to the process, to be flexible, and to accept his or her responsibilities along with rights in the same way other employees do.

This isn't the final support. What if the individual wants to move on? As with all other workers, even if they are happy with their work, clients may consider a move to further their career or for other reasons. They may want to develop and change their job from a safe and secure one to one which is perhaps less secure. This may happen after the move to unsupported employment, or even on the eve of such a progression.

You have to accept this in the face of overwhelming evidence that it would be a risk to their continued employment. We all take such risks and if the individual is made aware of the risks, as clearly and unambiguously as possible, but still wishes to proceed, then you will need to consider whether your service is able to restart the process again. Back to page 1 and copy the blank forms!

However, we are at the stage when the move to unsupported employment is imminent and you need to make sure that both employee and employer are aware of the steps leading to the complete fading of your support.

- Final meeting – review and agree part four of the Development Plan.

- Complete actions and objectives or have a close completion date.

- Resolve all support issues.

- Make both parties aware that you will continue to offer advice and support after the move to unsupported employment.

- Set a date for the post-progression meeting if desired.

- Confirm contact information.

- Set the final date for the move to unsupported employment.

- Confirm the date in writing, getting signatures of agreement from both parties.

Post-progression review

If a review meeting has been requested by the employee and employer and a date arranged you will need to be prepared.

- Review all the information you have on the process from the original initial contact through to the move to unsupported employment.

- Consider all the gaps that were dealt with. Is there anything that may resurface? Could you offer any further advice if this happens?

- Consider all the other issues that arose. Is there anything that could need further support? How could you help?

- Contact the employee independently and discuss the past few weeks. Have there been any problems? Is he or she still happy with the job? Is he or she managing financially; socially; emotionally?

- Contact the employer independently and discuss the past few weeks. Have they been monitoring progress? Do they have an appraisal system? (If so, it may be advisable to wait until this has taken place before arranging a meeting.)

- Feel confident that you have as much up-to-date information as there is available and ideas in mind for supporting any potential problems.

- Consider the possibility that there are other support options, including support from another more appropriate local agency. Contact them to discuss a possible collaboration. External training may be an option. Have you any funding to help with this?

- Remember that this process can work for anyone with a disability.

- Finally, prepare for the unexpected!

Asperger syndrome and supported employment

My thanks to Pat Baldwin, Manager of Workable, a supported employment service in Bradford, for this section on the effectiveness of using this strategy for people with a developmental disability.

Asperger syndrome is a disability that is highly individual, often hidden, and potentially debilitating for the person who has been assessed as having the condition. As a lifelong developmental disability, Asperger syndrome is a Pervasive Developmental Disorder (PDD) that can seriously impede an individual's ability to communicate and relate to other people socially, and it therefore creates great difficulties for the individual throughout years of education and in adult life, with all the transitional hurdles that life can bring. It is important to stress that every person with Asperger syndrome has a unique personality that has been shaped by individual life experiences (just as we all have).

Unlike people with autism, those with Asperger syndrome are less likely to have additional learning difficulties, have more pronounced motor deficits, onset seems to be later, and social deficits are present without grossly impaired speech and language (Frith 1991).

The psychological basis of autism and Asperger syndrome is still not clearly understood. The developing nervous system may be adversely influenced at an early stage by the effects of a variety of conditions such as maternal rubella, tuberous sclerosis, lack of oxygen at birth, cough, allergies and measles. Genetic factors appear significant, and metabolic abnormalities, or mineral and vitamin deficiencies may also be implicated among contributory causal factors.

People with autism have major problems in three areas known as The Triad of Impairments and share a common need for a structured and organised daily programme to help them cope with the demands of life.

1. Communication – autistic children nearly always start to talk late, if at all, in severe cases. Their progress with speech is often slow and sometimes quite odd. They may have difficulty understanding what other people say, and may seem not to notice when people talk to them.

2. Socialisation – autistic people lack awareness of other people, may not respond to other people or may respond oddly.

3. Imagination – autistic children rarely have much pretend play; they tend to concentrate on the physical properties of things, preferring to look at things from odd angles, line them up, tap or spin them. They are not usually able to play interactively with other children.

Obsessive interests, e.g. trains, vacuum cleaners, washing machines or timetables, play a major part in the life of a person within the spectrum. There is a great insistence by the individuals concerned that certain activities are carried out exactly the same way every time. Rituals play a large part in the everyday activity of a person within the spectrum. Many children and adults become very upset, angry and destructive if their usual routine is disrupted. In fact change has major consequences on those that are at the severe end of the spectrum.

People within the autistic spectrum are not alone in facing difficulties and setbacks with employment. For many individuals with any form of disability the chances of finding employment in the open market can be extremely difficult and limited if the correct support and guidance is not available. However, it has been demonstrated over the last ten years that, providing the correct support and details are in place, people with learning disabilities can enter the labour market successfully and be included in the workforce and society in general as a fully contributing individual. Unfortunately, until recently, many of these opportunities have been denied to young people within the autistic spectrum.

Often these young individuals are seen as having behavioural problems, as being strange, elusive, rude, abrupt, extrovert, odd, loners, socially inept and lacking in discipline. However, it is often the system that is creating this perceived monster, that is not supporting and assisting these young people correctly to stimulate and enhance an already high level of intelligence.

As stated earlier, these are the forgotten or misunderstood individuals that will eventually join our prospective workforce – if they are given the correct support and understanding at an early age to provide them with coping strategies for a world that they see as different and odd. In this way they have the potential to become valued and committed members of society.

The introduction of supported employment and a 'person-centred planning' process can address the needs of these young school-leavers, giving them the opportunity to gain employment and earn money, whilst entering adulthood and establishing a more separate lifestyle combined with independence.

Services designed for accommodating and counteracting specific learning disabilities may not address the range of problem areas in Asperger syndrome, especially when deficits are subtle, cause few problems for school officials, and do not directly and obviously impact on academic achievement. This results in a service provision that is not based on 'person-centred' planning, focusing on the needs of the individual, but that has a functional basis, planned by curriculum, and available resources are often missing the essential support and training required to meet the social and communication deficits that are inherent in a person within the autistic spectrum.

Understandably, those with Asperger syndrome experience enormous difficulties during transition into adolescence, and later into adult life, since they have not completed the requisite developmental tasks or moved beyond early stages in language, cognitive and social skills. They frequently remain emotionally dependent upon parents or family members, and suffer from separation anxiety and insecurity when trying to live on their own. Friendships with peers, romantic relationships, marriage and parenting, and entry into the 'world of work' are usually beyond their capacity. They remain, in many debilitating ways, stuck in time, trapped in the Asperger syndrome puzzle. They are, in essence, childlike beings attempting to live in the adult world, but without the support and understanding that children are afforded.

It is estimated that there are approximately 18,000 adults with autism in the UK who have average/above-average intellectual ability, but only around 20–25% are likely to be employed, and occupational status, even amongst those in jobs, is very low (Goode, Howlin and Rutter, 1993).

Person-centred planning and supported employment are the planning 'tools' that will enable disability employment professionals to assist an Asperger syndrome person in the transition into employment. Supported employment offers people with developmental disabilities the opportunity and the means to find and remain in employment with the assistance of professional staff that take into account the necessary support requirements of each prospective worker. Support, whether that of a natural co-worker or of a designated job trainer, may be the means to positively structuring the person's working day and routines so that the social and communication deficits that are commonly experienced by this client group are minimised. At the same time, support is available in a moment of uncertainty and change. See Case Study 7.1.

Case Study 7.1

James, diagnosed with Asperger syndrome at the age of 13, left a mainstream school at 19 and was supported through his upper school by a support assistant, who assisted him for 21 hours a week. He left school with a distinction in BTEC intermediate Business Administration and six GCSEs at Grade C and above. A referral from the careers office led him to a supported employment agency that followed the same principles as outlined throughout this publication. Efficient and effective profiling by the employment specialist ensured that skills and abilities, strengths and goals were identified alongside the autistic rituals and traits that were particular to him. Difficulties controlling breathing and speaking without gulping were recognisable manifestations of his disability. Hand-flapping and obvious signs of being distraught were displayed if he became emotionally distressed and was unable to function effectively. Over many informal meetings at James' home a relationship was established and a working profile identified that led to an understanding of need for employment. Identification of his specialist skills in remembering data, i.e. postcodes, and the support mechanism that was required (particularly to assist in times of distress when out of the ordinary experiences would trigger the hand-flapping rituals that James experienced in times of stress) were made to enable a successful job match to take place. An active job search with James together with social and communication-skills training led him to an interview at a large building society that was looking for additional workers for its post room. An offer of employment followed, and meetings took place between the job developer, James, the employer, the agency and James' mother that ensured that the best possible support could be given to James at the start of his employment. Constant updates and intervention were given to and from all parties, the employer very eager to learn and assist James. James is still in employment three years down the line with natural support in place from the semi-retired staff who also work in the post room. His confidence has developed to such an extent that he can now walk into all departments with the mail and say 'good morning' to other people. This would never have been envisaged in the early stages of his employment. The supported employment profiling and job-matching strategy is an efficient and effective method based on a 'person-centred' planning process that fulfils the needs of the individual and those of the employer.

James is just one of many young people who are desperate to enter the world of employment yet need the patience, understanding and equality of opportunity that is rightly theirs to enable them to 'cross the bridge' into independence.

Standardised assessment tests typically underrate the abilities of workers within the spectrum. A supported employment profiling and job-matching process enables the identification of specific skills, knowledge, expertise and abilities that can be developed to reduce social and communication deficits, enhancing already high skill levels and aiding employment. Identification of preferred learning styles, 'needs-led' training programmes and identification of requisite work skills with support mechanisms in place to assist in moments of change enhances job opportunities. In-depth profiling enables the employer to match up essential work skills and abilities to a role within the workplace, ensuring an almost perfect matching of skills that best utilises the expertise of the individual and maximises his or her contribution to the company.

Supported employment and person-centred profiling does work for people within the autistic spectrum.

Mental health and supported employment

My thanks to Dave Willingham and Catherine Felce for this section on the use of supported employment for people with enduring mental health problems.

When discussing the issues surrounding employment and mental health, we must first consider the frequently asked question, 'How can you justify supporting someone to find work when it was employment that caused their mental health problems?'

It is important to understand that there are many employment situations that could have triggered the problem. Employment is not one particular scenario with one definition, but is made up of many elements, and has a different meaning and purpose for each of us.

Factors that have been found to determine positive mental health in the workplace are:

1.   Financial reward

2.   Valued social position

3.   Variety of activities

4.   Clarity of cultural and work related aspects of the work environment.

5.   Development of social relationships

6. Degree of autonomy

7. Opportunity to use skills

8. Physical security

(Hill 2000)

The vocational profiling process can help the individual understand what order of priority these factors should be in for them to achieve a positive working environment. For example, a person may place greater emphasis on the opportunity to use skills than the development of social relationships or on job security over autonomy.

Therefore, we should not attribute the whole job to the illness but try to identify which specific elements caused the problems. Everyone reacts differently to the various events thrown at them during their lives, and this includes illnesses and their subsequent treatment.

Only by understanding the person, can we journey along the road of successful and sustainable employment. The processes outlined in this workbook clearly give an opportunity for the individual and SE practitioner to identify the specific aspects likely to be the cause of any recurrence of previous problems.

Mental health problems are almost invariably seen as problems to be overcome. Supported employment gives people an opportunity to access employment despite their difficulties, rather than spending a considerable amount of time feeling isolated and unemployable until they have fully recovered.

An exercise recently used as part of a series of supported employment lectures in an Assertive Outreach modular course, given to mental health professionals throughout the UK in 2001 (Teesside University, Derbyshire School of Health and Tulip Mental Health Trust), posed two questions to the audience:

1. What is employment?

2. What is illness?

The idea behind question 1 was to encourage people to think about what employment meant to them personally. Examples of the responses were:

- Finance

- Independence

- Self-worth

- Self respect

- Security

- Reason for getting out of bed
- Meet people

In question 2, people were asked how they perceived illness; what they associated with it, and how they would feel if they became ill, particularly over a long period of time. Some of the responses to this were:

- Isolation
- Medication
- Loss of self-esteem
- Helplessness
- Desire to be well again
- Financial difficulty

By comparing the responses to both questions it can be seen that meaningful employment could actually reduce some of the difficulties people face when they are ill, regardless of the nature of the illness. This exercise highlights the potential benefits of employment, providing appropriate support is given and preparatory work completed.

All this information should be collected during the profiling process to enable people to relate to their own experiences and aspirations, resulting in a clear path to a good job match. Additional aspects, including training needs, emotional support, travel, and benefits issues, can be highlighted. Most importantly, potential pitfalls can be identified and eliminated from the job-finding process.

'Risk' is another common concern amongst professionals and employers. Risks are part of life and people should be permitted to make their own choices and take their own risks. SE practitioners must identify the risks associated with each individual employment opportunity, working with their clients to ensure they are able to make informed choices. Individuals should be supported through their choices and where necessary given assistance to resolve problems or rectify mistakes.

Risk assessments should be provided by an individual's care co-ordinator to enable the SE practitioner to use it as a tool to help identify areas of concern and work with the clients to minimise them. Risk assessments should not be used to exclude people from employment.

The majority of people with mental health problems who access supported employment are quite often experiencing severe and enduring mental health problems. The processes in this workbook are extremely useful to SE practitioners when working with such clients. The work is akin to that of professionals working in

Assertive Outreach teams or those who provide similar services. The commonalities that exist between the services are that they are:

- multi-disciplinary (various expertise)

- flexible

- provided in community setting, e.g. persons have place of employment, places of recreation, rather than an office setting.

- adapting processes to the individual rather than specific policies and procedures

- provided indefinitely.

   (US General Accounting Office 2000)

Studies in the USA suggest that various interventions such as supported employment, especially when a person begins to experience difficulties, can:

1.   reduce hospital admissions

2.   reduce length of hospital stays

3.   improve social functioning

4.   improve house stability

5.   reduce symptoms of thought disorder and unusual behaviours.

(Mental Health Foundation 1999)

The approach used in this workbook is generic and can be transferred to anyone experiencing difficulties accessing the open labour market as it focuses on the person and not his or her illness or disability.

   Supported employment should be used more widely to include work interventions, so that people who develop mental health problems whilst still in employment can get support earlier. This early intervention, backed up with a sound knowledge of employment and employment law, can substantially reduce the chances of people losing jobs.

   Work is a fundamentally important factor in the life of every adult of working age and is a major factor in promoting mental health (Perkins 1997). Consequently, successful supported employment interventions can help reduce the risk of the illness becoming more serious.

Final conclusion

You have made it to the end of the workbook and, hopefully, the client has made it into unsupported employment, but don't be surprised or too disappointed if this is not the case.

By using this workbook and the comprehensive strategy in it, you will have increased your chances of delivering a supported employment service that gets positive results. It is sad to say, however, that, given present statistical probabilities regarding a move to unsupported employment for people with disabilities, your chance of success is at best evens.

You must not let this dishearten you, because ten years ago your chance of such an outcome would have been much smaller. We are improving our success rate as we become more experienced, more confident in our service being able to deliver results, and more aware of the principles behind supported employment. We are making the option of unsupported employment a realistic goal for people who would not have been given that choice ten years ago.

You are also acting as a beacon of good practice for all organisations that are involved in people-centred services and for employers, who are beginning to see that supported employment services are not coming cap in hand for charitable donations but are offering an excellent service that looks to their needs as well as the needs of the individual. You will have a service that believes in making a commitment to strengthening the relationship between employee and employer, and doesn't go for short-term success at the expense of long-term sustainability.

Using this process does not lead you to a dead end; if you are unsuccessful you will have generated a great deal of useful information about what went wrong. This can be used when you restart the process, and you will have the experience and information to avoid the pitfalls from your first plan.

If you use this workbook in a developmental and flexible way to build your service around the principles of supported employment then you will have begun to make changes that will have repercussions throughout the country.

As more people succeed a groundswell of disenfranchised people will begin to ask the question, 'Why can't I access such a supported employment service?', and the government will have to listen and maybe they will 'learn and move on'.

steve.leach@scope.org.uk

Appendix 1a

Initial Contact Form		Client name:	
Client address:			
Town:		Postcode:	
Telephone:		Email:	
Date of birth:		NI no:	
Unemployed:	Yes/No	If yes, length of time:	
Meeting arranged	Time:	Date:	Venue:
Other details (advocate requested, special requirements, access, communicator etc.):			
Disability:			
Referral source	[ ] Self	[ ] DEA	[ ] Employer	[ ] Other
Details	Name:		
Organisation:			
Address:			
Town:		Postcode:	
Telephone:		Email:	
Employer details:	If referrer is not the [potential] employer are any details available?		
Organisation:			
Address:			
Town:		Postcode:	
Telephone:		Email:	
Contact name:		Position:	
Action planned or other information (issues, concerns, potential supports):			

Appendix 1b

Initial Contact Form	Client name: *Jane Jones*

Client address: *84 Nanfield Drive*	
Town: *Egham*	Postcode: *EG44 GG55*
Telephone: *01234 567890*	Email:
Date of birth: *18/04/67*	NI no: *PP 12 34 56 P*

Unemployed:	Yes/~~No~~	If yes, length of time: *4 years*	
Meeting arranged	Time: 3pm	Date: 24/04/00	Venue: job centre

Other details (advocate requested, special requirements, access, communicator etc.) : *Jane decided that her friend, Joan, knew her well and would help her explain what she wanted. She has full use of her limbs but a sight impairment means that she needs documents in large print.*

Disability: *Cerebral palsy, visual impairment*

Referral source	[X] Self	[ ] DEA	[ ] Employer	[ ] Other
Details	Name: *Jim Jackson*			

Organisation: *Employment Service*	
Address: *Jamestown Road*	
Town: *Egham*	Postcode: *EG33 GG44*
Telephone: *04321 0987656*	Email:

Employer details:	If referrer is not the [potential] employer are any details available
Organisation:	
Address:	
Town:	Postcode:
Telephone:	Email:
Contact name:	Position:

Action planned or other information (issues, concerns, potential supports):

Telecon 12/4/00 Jane has been at college for the past two years learning business administration (successfully completed HND Bus. Studies) and would like to look for appropriate work. Has written for many jobs without success. She feels, as a wheelchair user, that her disability is having a negative effect on her interview chances. Whilst she has a clear idea of the field of work she is less clear about any particular job and would be grateful for some support with this as well. We discussed the idea of profiling and job matching and she felt this would be useful. I will send her a copy of the profile in large print format and Jane will discuss this with her friend in readiness for the meeting.

Appendix 2a

The Vocational Profile	
Client Name:	
Address:	
Town:	Postcode:
Telephone:	Email:
Date of birth:	NI no:

Vocational profiling is an approach to self-assessment that gathers information about individual aims, experiences and aspirations to achieve a successful job match and, therefore, long-term sustainable employment. It is not about judging your potential for obtaining employment. Anyone who wants to work can work with the right support.

Information contained in the profile should be based on your whole life, and not just taken from a sample of your work performance.

Please complete the profile as fully as possible, telling us about yourself and the things that interest you, and then we will review all the information. Use extra sheets whenever necessary – keep writing!

1. **Life Experiences** (residential/community)

Consider things like:

- people living with you, how long been there
- what you do during the day/in the evening
- what jobs you can do at home – cooking, cleaning, gardening
- sorts of places you like/dislike
- what would be good about getting a job
- anything you think might help us find a job that suits you.

This is about *you* and the job that you might like to do, so please complete as fully as possible.

Continue on to the following page or add any extra sheets if you need more space.

A SUPPORTED EMPLOYMENT WORKBOOK

Life Experiences (continued)

Life Experiences (continued)

2. Educational Information/Academic Skills: What schools did you go to? Any certificates achieved? Other courses done?	
CV available: Yes/No	Attached: Yes/No

3. Work experience Information (Current and most recent past)

Most recent job:	How long?: Hours/week:

Duties (brief details but try to list all duties for future discussions):

Why did you leave this job?

What did you like about this job?

What did you dislike about this job?

2. Next recent job:	How long?: Hours/week:

Duties (brief details but try to list all duties for future discussions):

Why did you leave this job?

What did you like about this job?

What did you dislike about this job?

4. What Job Would You Like to Do Now?

5. Workplace Flexibility Requirements (e.g. ground floor, close supervisor, machinery limited)

Habits, routines, temperament (e.g. one task only, talks a lot, needs support, set breaks):

Physical/Health/Mobility needs (e.g. sitting, no stairs):

Sorts of things you like to do (e.g. repetitive, factory, office, computer, teams):

Sorts of things you dislike doing:

Behavioural challenges (e.g. easily angered/frustrated, talks incessantly, overemotional)

Any other information that you think might be helpful:

6. Employee Skills/Preferences (matches up to the job analysis grid)

This grid identifies your work preferences and skills. A mark in box 1 indicates your clear preference for the statement on the left of the scale, a mark in box 9 indicates a clear preference on the right of the scale, and a mark in box 5 indicates no preference or average skill in that area.

Add any skills/preferences to the list that you feel are relevant. Add any narrative on the grid or using a continuation sheet that will offer clarity and help with the job-matching process.

The intention is to match your responses to the job analysis grid from the employer and identify potential job matches. It will not be used to exclude you from any work so please be accurate.

Preferences

I like to work…

	1	2	3	4	5	6	7	8	9	
full time										part time (<16 hours)
indoors										outdoors
staying in one place										moving about
in a busy workplace										in a relaxed workplace
in a hot workplace										in a cold workplace
in a noisy workplace										in a quiet workplace
in a clean workplace										in a messy workplace
constantly – one job										doing different tasks
in a big workplace										in a small workplace
mainly with men										mainly with women
in a uniform										without a uniform
with words/books										not with words
with numbers										not with numbers
using public transport										not using public transport
with others										not with others

Please add any other preferences you feel are relevant

153

	1	2	3	4	5	6	7	8	9	
I can use my hands										I can't use my hands
I have good eyesight										I have a visual impairment
I have good hearing										I have poor hearing
I communicate well										I can't communicate well
I can lift heavy loads										I don't like heavy lifting
I have stamina										I don't have stamina
I can read										I can't read
I can use numbers										I can't use numbers
I can use money										I can't use money
I can tell time										I can't tell time
I can work quickly										I can't work quickly
I can achieve quality										I can't achieve quality
I can concentrate >2hrs										I can't concentrate >2hrs
I can do varied tasks										I can do 1-2 tasks only
I have good balance										I don't have good balance
I can walk										I cannot walk
I can stand for >2hrs										I cannot stand for >2hrs
I can sit for>2hrs										I cannot sit for >2hrs
I can use stairs										I cannot use stairs
I don't often get angry										I often get angry
I can remember instructions										I cannot remember instructions
I can use the phone										I cannot use the phone
I can drive										I cannot drive
I can use a computer										I cannot use a computer
I can spell										I cannot spell
I have good handwriting										I can't write well
I can use my judgement										I can't use my judgement
I can work without support										I cannot work without direct support
I can use my initiative										I can't use my initiative
I can look after my appearance										I have difficulty looking after my appearance
I have good personal hygiene										I don't have good personal hygiene
Add any other skills that you feel are important to you										

7. Support Needs Checklist (Write in last column which code number most accurately reflects your support needs)		Enter code below 1 = Need full support 2 = Need some support
General	**Evidence/information/examples**	3 = No support needed
Timekeeping		
Attendance		
Communication		
Behaviour		
Dress/appearance		
Social interaction		
Work-related skills		
Motivation		
Flexibility		
Initiative		
Team-skills		
Health and Saftey		
Consistency		
Working under pressure		
Work tasks (identified in job description, if applicable, i.e. only when a particular job is identified or the client is already in employment)		
a)		
b)		
c)		
d)		
e)		
f)		
g)		
h)		
Comments:		
Review date agreed:		

8. Personal Disability Information

Disability/impairment (self-description and any supporting information). This information is important for us to understand how best support can be arranged to achieve a successful job match. Explanation of how the disability, condition or mental impairment affects you and how it could impact on the work situation will be very useful for this purpose. Please be as accurate and comprehensive as possible.

Secondary conditions? E.g.:		Details
Epilepsy	yes/no	
Hepatitis B	yes/no	
Visual impairment	yes/no	
Asthma	yes/no	
Diabetes	yes/no	
Bronchitis	yes/no	
Dermatitis	yes/no	
Eczema	yes/no	
Speech impairment	yes/no	
Heart condition	yes/no	
Deafness	yes/no	
Other	yes/no	
On medication?	yes/no	

If yes, please give details, particularly if there are side effects that may impact on work:

Other relevant health information (allergies etc.):

Doctor (GP):	Phone no.:
Consultant:	Phone no.:
Notes: Medical information requested	Yes/No (if yes, attach medical permission letter)

Other comments:

9. Benefits Information

Try and enter all information – it may influence the decision regarding employment – pre-work and in-work benefits information is also important.

Are you in receipt of any of the following benefits?

		Position now	Position in employment
J.S.A (inc. disablity premium)	yes/no	£	N/a
Incapacity Benefit – high rate, short term	yes/no	£	N/a
Incapacity Benefit – long term	yes/no	£	N/a
Income Support (inc. disability premium)	yes/no	£	£
Severe Disability Allowance	yes/no	£	N/a
D.L.A. care component	yes/no	£	£
D.L.A. mobility component	yes/no	£	£
Housing Benefit	yes/no	£	£
Council Tax Relief	yes/no	£	£
Total benefits/allowances		£	£
Wages	yes/no		
Other income	yes/no		

Details: (e.g. on a government training scheme)

D.W.A./DPTC	yes/no	£	£
Do you have a spouse or partner?	yes/no		
Spouse/Partner's earning and income:		£	
Do you have any dependent children?:	yes/no		
If yes, number of children?		Ages:	

Other information (savings, income, trusts, house owner, who else gets benefits etc.):

Total income/benefits pre-employment =	£	per wk/mnth
Total income/benefits in employment =	£	per wk/mnth
Total income increase/decrease	£	per wk/mnth

Comments:

Letter of permission signed:	yes/no	Date:

10. Information Analysis/Review This is where all the information is collated from the VP process and potential future development routes, based on that information and discussion with the client, are formulated to be included in the Development Plan Part One. Both job developer (JD) and potential employee should complete this review and sign it.

What are the main points to be drawn from the profile information?

i. What sorts of jobs are identified?

ii. What are the work/personal support needs?

iii. Any learning/development needs identified?

iv. Potential development route?

v. What are the immediate objectives? (Transfer these in detail to the Development Plan)

vi. What is the client going to do to support his/her job search?

vii. What is the JD going to do to support the client's job search?

(I agree that the information given above can be kept on a computer database and used to support my job match)

Signature

Employee:

Job Developer:

Date:

Appendix 2b

The Vocational Profile

Client Name: *A. N. Other*

Address: *Anytown Street*

Town: *Anytown*	Postcode: *AT11 T22*
Telephone: *01234 567890*	Email:
Date of birth: *16/04/64*	NI no: *AT 12 34 56 T*

Vocational profiling is an approach to self-assessment that gathers information about individual aims, experiences and aspirations to achieve a successful job match and, therefore, long-term sustainable employment. It is not about judging your potential for obtaining employment. Anyone who wants to work can work with the right support.

Information contained in the profile should be based on your whole life, and not just taken from a sample of your work performance.

Please complete the profile as fully as possible, telling us about yourself and the things that interest you, and then we will review all the information. Use extra sheets whenever necessary – keep writing!

1. Life experiences (residential/community)

Consider things like:

- people living with you, how long been there
- what you do during the day/in the evening
- what jobs you can do at home – cooking, cleaning, gardening
- sorts of places you like/dislike
- what would be good about getting a job
- anything you think might help us find a job that suits you.

This is about you and the job that you might like to do, so please complete as fully as possible.

Continue on to the following page or add any extra sheets if you need more space.

For about 10 years or so I have worked with my father running a small nursery/garden centre. In between work and in the evenings I have enjoyed looking after my animals and birds.

In my spare time I watch TV and enjoy films and wildlife programmes.

I have always lived at home with my mother. My father died last year and we had to sell the business. I have one brother who lives close by. My uncle who has helped us a lot lives away in the south but visits regularly.

We have now moved. I have had little work since moving.

I have an allotment where I keep my chickens and grow vegetables.

At home I help keep the garden tidy and look after my cat.

I often wash up and make drinks and I have sometimes cooked breakfast.

I would like a job to keep me occupied and to earn some money.

The ideal job for me would be in horticulture – growing and selling.

I have some knowledge about growing and it gives me real satisfaction to grow something and then sell it.

2. Educational information/Academic skills: What school did you go to? Any certificates achieved? Other courses done?

I went to Spring Garden Upper School for children with special needs. I achieved a City & Guilds Certificate in Horticulture.

I have trouble reading and with maths but get by and can recognise words, particularly related to plants and wildlife.

CV available:	~~Yes~~/No	Attached:	Yes/No

3. Work experience Information (Current and most recent past)

Most recent job: *Self-employed*	How long?: *10 yrs*	Hours/week: *40*

Duties (brief details but try to list all duties for future discussions):

Potting plants, including evergreens and alpines. Watering and general tidying up. I helped sell the plants at our garden centre and at agricultural shows and markets.

Why did you leave this job?

My father died and we had to sell the business.

What did you like about this job?

I worked for myself and enjoyed growing and selling plants. I learned a lot about plants. I enjoy being outdoors.

What did you dislike about this job?

I did not like wet and cold weather. I did not like difficult customers.

2. Next recent job: *None*	How long?:	Hours/week:

Duties (brief details but try to list all duties for future discussions):

Why did you leave this job?

What did you like about this job?

What did you dislike about this job?

4. What Job Would You Like to Do Now?
I would like to work in a garden centre or nursery, helping growing and selling plants.

5. Workplace Flexibility Requirements (e.g. ground floor, close supervisor, machinery limited)
I am physically able. *I would prefer some supervision.* *I can use simple machinery.*

Habits routines, temerament (e.g. one task only, talks a lot, needs support, set breaks):
I prefer to concentrate on one job at a time. *I feel quite relaxed but I can get frustrated if continually harassed.* *I do need some encouragement and some supervision.*

Physical/Health/Mobility needs (sitting, no stairs):
I am physically able and have good health. I am rarely sick.

Sorts of things you like to do (e.g. repetitive, factory, office, computer, teams):
Horticulture is repetitive but I enjoy it, especially growing plants. *I am happy to work in a team, or on my own with supervision.*

Sorts of things you dislike doing:
I can think of nothing in horticulture I dislike doing.

Behavioural challenges (e.g. easily angered/frustrated, talks incessantly, overemotional)
I can get frustrated if harassed or challenged. *I can talk continually about my birds and animals if I have a willing audience.*

Any other information that you think might be helpful:
I live in a rural area and may need help in getting to and from a job. *My mother is willing to help and has lots of local contacts. She does work part-time so this will need to be managed carefully.* *I enjoy learning about plants and their history. I like to be shown how to do things and working alongside someone to pick things up. If they talk me through jobs as well as showing me in a patient way I learn best.*

6. Employee Skills/Preferences (matches up to the job analysis grid)

This grid identifies your work preferences and skills. A mark in box 1 indicates your clear preference for the statement on the left of the scale, a mark in box 9 indicates a clear preference on the right of the scale, and a mark in box 5 indicates no preference or average skill in that area.

Add any skills/preferences to the list that you feel are relevant. Add any narrative on the grid or using a continuation sheet that will offer clarity and help with the job-matching process.

The intention is to match your responses to the job analysis grid from the employer and identify potential job matches. It will not be used to exclude you from any work so please be accurate.

Preferences

I like to work...

	1	2	3	4	5	6	7	8	9	
full time							x			part time (<16 hours)
indoors							x			outdoors
staying in one place	x									moving about
in a busy workplace							x			in a relaxed workplace
in a hot workplace			x							in a cold workplace
in a noisy workplace							x			in a quiet workplace
in a clean workplace			x							in a messy workplace
constantly – one job							x			doing different tasks
in a big workplace							x			in a small workplace
mainly with men				x						mainly with women
in a uniform					x					without a uniform
with words/books									x	not with words
with numbers							x			not with numbers
using public transport				x						not using public transport
with others			x							not with others

Please add any other preferences you feel are relevant

	1	2	3	4	5	6	7	8	9	
with plants	x									
where I can talk to people		x								
not too far from home			x							

	1	2	3	4	5	6	7	8	9	
I can use my hands		x								I can't use my hands
I have good eyesight	x									I have a visual impairment
I have good hearing	x									I have poor hearing
I communicate well			x							I can't communicate well
I can lift heavy loads		x								I don't like heavy lifting
I have stamina				x						I don't have stamina
I can read						x				I can't read
I can use numbers						x				I can't use numbers
I can use money						x				I can't use money
I can tell time	x									I can't tell time
I can work quickly						x				I can't work quickly
I can achieve quality				x						I can't achieve quality
I can concentrate >2hrs							x			I can't concentrate >2hrs
I can do varied tasks					x					I can do 1-2 tasks only
I have good balance			x							I don't have good balance
I can walk	x									I cannot walk
I can stand for >2hrs	x									I cannot stand for >2hrs
I can sit for >2hrs	x									I cannot sit for >2hrs
I can use stairs	x									I cannot use stairs
I don't often get angry								x		I often get angry
I can remember instructions				x						I cannot remember instructions
I can use the phone	x									I cannot use the phone
I can drive								x		I cannot drive
I can use a computer							x			I cannot use a computer
I can spell						x				I cannot spell
I have good handwriting						x				I can't write well
I can use my judgement			x							I can't use my judgement
I can work without direct support					x					I cannot work without direct support
I can use my initiative					x					I can't use my initiative
I can look after my appearance					x					I have difficulty looking after my appearance
I have good personal hygiene					x					I don't have good personal hygiene

Add any other skills that you feel are important to you

	1	2	3	4	5	6	7	8	9	
I can look after animals		x								
I have my own allotment		x								

7. Support Needs Checklist		Enter code below
(Write in last column which code number most accurately reflects your support needs)		1 = Need full support
		2 = Need some support
General	**Evidence/information/examples**	3 = No support needed
Timekeeping	*I like to be on time for appointments*	2
Attendance	*I am very conscientious*	2
Communication	*I enjoy talking to people*	2
Behaviour	*I am usually quiet*	2
Dress/appearance	*I like my gardening clothes*	2
Social interaction	*I am quiet but like company*	2
Work-related skills		
Motivation	*I can get sidetracked and need some support*	2
Flexability	*I enjoy doing all gardening jobs*	2
Initiative	*I know when to plant out and weed*	2
Team-skills	*I have always worked with others*	2
Health and Safety	*I wear safety shoes and won't use chemicals unless someone is there*	2
Consistency	*I can plant out a whole patch*	2
Working under pressure	*I don't like pressure as I get confused and forget some jobs*	2

Work tasks (identified in job description, if applicable, i.e. only when a particular job is identified or the client is already in employment)	
a) Planting out	*3*
b) Digging	*3*
c) Picking fruit	*2*
d) Hoeing	*3*
e) Edging borders	*2*
f) Pruning	*2*
g) Grass cutting	*2*
h) Weeding	*3*
I) Digging up vegetables	*3*
j) Cutting flowers	*3*
k)	

Comments:

Review date agreed:

8. Personal Disability Information

Disability/impairment (self-description and any supporting information). This information is important for us to understand how best support can be arranged to achieve a successful job match. Explanation of how the disability, condition or mental impairment affects you and how it could impact on the work situation will be very useful for this purpose. Please be as accurate and comprehensive as possible.

I have some learning difficulties and can get confused if people are impatient with me. I like to take my time and watch how other people do things. I have difficulty with written words and numbers but can hold conversations with people, especially if they are talking about plants and animals. I can let things get on my mind and this can cause me to make mistakes or get upset but if I can talk about it I can usually get through it.

Secondary conditions? E.g.:		Details
Epilepsy	~~yes~~/no	
Hepatitis B	~~yes~~/no	
Visual impairment	~~yes~~/no	
Asthma	~~yes~~/no	
Diabetes	~~yes~~/no	
Bronchitis	~~yes~~/no	
Dermatitis	~~yes~~/no	
Eczema	~~yes~~/no	
Speech impairment	yes/~~no~~	*Minor and is quite eloquent*
Heart condition	~~yes~~/no	
Deafness	~~yes~~/no	
Other	~~yes~~/no	
On medication?	~~yes~~/no	

If yes, please give details, particularly if there are side effects that may impact on work:

Other relevant health information (allergies etc.):
None

Doctor (GP): *Dr K.*	Phone no.:
Consultant:	Phone no.:
Notes: Medical information requested	~~Yes~~/No (if yes, attach medical permission letter)

Other comments:

9. Benefits information

Try and enter all information – it may influence the decision regarding employment – pre-work and in-work benefits information, is also important.

Are you in receipt of any of the following benefits?

		Position now	Position in employment
J.S.A (inc. disability premium)	~~yes~~/no	£	N/a
Incapacity Benefit – high rate, short term	~~yes~~/no	£	N/a
Incapacity Benefit – long term	~~yes~~/no	£	N/a
Income Support (inc. disability premium)	~~yes~~/no	£	£
Severe Disability Allowance	~~yes~~/no	£	N/a
D.L.A. care component	~~yes~~/no	£	£
D.L.A. mobility component	yes/~~no~~	£56 per month	£
Housing Benefit	~~yes~~/no	£	£
Council Tax Relief	~~yes~~/no	£	£
Total benefits/allowances		£56 per month	£
Wages	~~yes~~/no		
Other income	~~yes~~/no		

Details: (e.g. on a government training scheme)

D.W.A./DPTC	~~yes~~/no	£	£
Do you have a spouse or partner?	~~yes~~/no		
Spouse/Partner's earning and income:		£	
Do you have any dependent children?	~~yes~~/no		
If yes, number of children?		Ages:	

Other information (savings, income, trusts, house owner, who else gets benefits etc.):

I am half owner of my home
I have >£5000 in savings
I owe £2000 in tax

Total income/benefits pre-employment =	£56	per ~~wk~~/mnth
Total income/benefits in employment =	£	per wk/mnth
Total income increase/decrease	£	per wk/mnth

Comments:

I have not claimed job seeker's allowance but I am going to see the disability adviser next week.

Letter of permission signed:	yes/no	Date:

10. Information Analysis/Review

This is where all the information is collated from the VP process and potential future development routes, based on that information and discussion with the client, are formulated to be included in the Development Plan Part One. Both job developer (JD) and potential employee should complete this review and sign it.

What are the main points to be drawn from the profile information?

---

i. What sorts of jobs are identified?

- *National Trust Sites Parks and Gardens*
- *Local Estates Gardening and landscaping*
- *Open Farms*
- *Bird and Wildlife Sanctuaries*

---

ii. What are the work/personal support needs?

- *Chris needs close support in the initial stages of any new job.*
- *If there are a variety of tasks then Chris will need support to concentrate on one job at a time – a clear work schedule will be important.*
- *A small team base would be helpful so that Chris can begin to adjust to a new environment and gain confidence.*
- *Some repetitive jobs would be useful for Chris to establish himself.*

---

iii. Any learning/development needs identified?

- *Chris will need close support to learn any new job.*
- *Chris will need help in setting targets and prioritising.*
- *Chris will need a great deal of encouragement and positive reinforcement to progress.*
- *A job supporter may be appropriate depending on the particular work environment.*

---

iv. Potential development route?

- *Chris has enormous potential and in the right supportive environment will have a lot to contribute.*
- *Chris is conscientious and knowledgeable in all aspects of nursery work.*
- *Chris is enthusiastic and willing to learn.*
- *Chris needs close support and sensitive encouragement to progress.*
- *Chris wants to achieve a greater level of independence for himself and full-time employment is an important key to this goal.*

What are the immediate objectives? (Transfer these in detail to the Development Plan)

See the Development Plan part one – Appendix 4b

What is the client going to do to support his/her job search?

See the Development Plan part one – Appendix 4b

What is the JD going to do to support the client's job search?

See the Development Plan part one – Appendix 4b

(I agree that the information given above can be kept on a computer database and used to support my job match)

Signature

Employee:

Job Developer:

Date:

Appendix 3

Vocational Profile Preference Grid (partially completed)

Employee Skills/Preferences (matches up to the job analysis grid)

This grid identifies your work preferences and skills. A mark in box 1 indicates your clear preference for the statement on the left of the scale, a mark in box 9 indicates a clear preference on the right of the scale, and a mark in box 5 indicates no preference or average skill in that area.

Add any skills/preferences to the list that you feel are relevant. Add any narrative on the grid or using a continuation sheet that will offer clarity and help with the job-matching process.

The intention is to match your responses to the job analysis grid from the employer and identify potential job matches. It will not be used to exclude you from any work so please be accurate.

Preferences										
I like to work...	1	2	3	4	5	6	7	8	9	
full time		x								part time (<16 hours)
indoors	x									outdoors
staying in one place								x		moving about
in a busy workplace					x					in a relaxed workplace
in a hot workplace			x							in a cold workplace
in a noisy workplace							x			in a quiet workplace
in a clean workplace	x									in a messy workplace
constantly – one job					x					doing different tasks
in a big workplace							x			in a small workplace
mainly with men					x					mainly with women
in uniform					x					without a uniform
with words/books								x		not with words
with numbers					x					not with numbers
using public transport	x									not using public transport
with others		x								not with others

Job Analysis Characteristics Grid

Employer Job Characteristics/Requirements (matches up to the vocational profile grid)										
The job is...	1	2	3	4	5	6	7	8	9	
full time					x					part time (<16 hours)
indoors		x								outdoors
staying in one place				x						moving about
in a busy workplace				x						in a relaxed workplace
in a hot work place			x							in a cold workplace
in a noisy workplace						x				in a quiet workplace
in a clean workplace			x							in a messy workplace
constantly – one job								x		doing different tasks
in a big workplace				x						in a small workplace
mainly with men					x					mainly with women
in uniform					x					without a uniform
with words/books								x		not with words
with numbers					x					not with numbers
using public transport					x					not using public transport
with others	x									not with others

Appendix 4a

Development Plan Part One

Client Name:

Indications of skills and preferences described in the vocational profile (VP) and any other relevant information available helps both the employee and employment officer identify areas for development. This may include proposing job tasters, further assessments (e.g. IT support) or job search plans. Future areas for development should be documented in the table below.

Summary of development plan for the client (summarise from the VP, section 10: Information Analysis Review, items 10i–10iv)

Objectives (collate from VP, section 10, items 10v–10vii)	By Whom	Start Date	Finish Date	Performance Indicator (How will the objective be completed)	Comments

Signed (Employee)   Date

Signed (Employment Officer):   Date   **Review Date:**

Development Plan Part Two

Client Name:

Indications of needs identified in the job-matching process (using the vocational profile and job analysis) help both the employee and employer identify areas for development. This may include proposing changes in the job itself, work environment, support mechanisms or the employee him/herself. Future areas for development should be documented in the table below.

Summary of job-matching information for the client (use the information from the VP and JA matching process)

Objectives	By Whom	Start Date	Finish Date	Performance Indicator (How will the objective be completed?)	Comments

Signed (Employee)   Date

Signed (Employment Officer):   Date   Review Date:

Development Plan Part Three

Client Name:

This is the result of the information from the Ongoing Support Review Process (3–6 months into employment) including the vocational profile, job analysis and any employer appraisal review available. This helps both the employee and employer identify areas for development. This may include proposing further changes in the job itself, work environment, support mechanisms or the employee themselves. Future areas of development should be documented in the table below.

Summary of the Ongoing Support Review for the client

Objectives	By Whom	Start Date	Finish Date	Performance Indicator (How will the objective be completed?)	Comments

Signed (Employee)   Date

Signed (Employment Officer):   Date   **Review Date:**

APPENDIX 4A

Development Plan Part Four

Client Name:

Full review of the supported employment process: vocational profile and job analysis review, Support Review Charts and any other relevant information (6–12 months from start of employment). This should include a plan for progression to unsupported employment. If not then undertake another Ongoing Support Review to aid further developments.

Summary of the Overall Job Review (OJR) for the client (use information from all previous reviews)

Objectives	By Whom	Start Date	Finish Date	Performance Indicator (How will the objective be completed?)	Comments

Signed (Employee)   Date

Signed (Employment Officer):   Date   Review Date:

Development Plan Part One

Client Name: *Chris Jonas*

Indications of skills and preferences described in the vocational profile (VP) and any other relevant information available helps both the employee and employment officer identify areas for development. This may include proposing job tasters, further assessments (e.g. IT support) or job search plans. Future areas for development should be documented in the table below.

Summary of development plan for the client (summarise from the VP, section 10: Information Analysis Review, items 10i–10iv)

To find a job for Chris that fulfils his aspirations and skills, based in the local area. The job should be permanent and long-term drawing on his skills in the market gardening field and his knowledge of bird and other wildlife.

Objectives (collate from VP, section 10, items 10v–10vii)	By Whom	Start Date	Finish Date	Performance Indicator (How will the objective be completed?)	Comments
To determine local job opportunities	*Chris, Job developer, DEA*	*Now*	*Ongoing*	*At least 10 potential job opportunities identified in next 2 weeks*	*This will be part of the review in 3 weeks' time*
Chris to continue to liaise with Southbridge Health Care, via Ray Jones	*Chris*	*Ongoing*	*N/a*	*Regular feedback from Chris and OT on progress*	*This relates to developing social skills in a work situation*
Meet the DEA	*Job developer*	*18/04/00*	*18/04/00*	*Specific job opportunities identified*	*Feed into review process*
Chris to undertake a job taster on local estate	*Chris/job developer*	*20/04/00*	*20/04/00*	*Clearer idea about job goal and any potential 'gaps'*	*Feed into review process*

Signed (Employee): *Chris Jonas* **Date:** *14/04/00*

Signed (Employment Officer): *Steve Leach* **Date:** *14/04/00* **Review Date:** *03/05/00*

Development Plan Part Two

Client Name: *Chris Jonas*

Indications of needs identified in the job-matching process (using the vocational profile and job analysis) help both the employee and employer identify areas for development. This may include proposing changes in the job itself, work environment, support mechanisms or the employee him/herself. Future areas for development should be documented in the table below.

Summary of job-matching information for the client (use the information from the VP and JA matching process)

This shows that with the support of the head gardener (HG) at Ouskirk Hall Chris will be able to undertake most tasks with a minimum of support. There are two tasks identified that will, because of their unsupported nature, need considerable input from the HG, who is also the natural work support. the environment and general nature of the tasks support the idea that this will be a very good match for Chris.

Objectives	By Whom	Start Date	Finish Date	Performance Indicator (How will the objective be completed?)	Comments
Consider how the two tasks can be modified to support Chris	*HG*	*Now*	*8 weeks*	*New job plan for these two tasks*	*I will work with the HG to advise on changes that can be made*
Consider the use of a job supporter for these two tasks	*Job developer*	*Now*	*4 weeks*	*Chris agreeing with this, identification of suitable person*	*Contact learning disability services who have offered help*
Draw up a full range of duties and the support needs for each task	*HG*	*Now*	*4 weeks*	*Chris will work exclusively with the HG for 2 hours every morning during the next 3 months on each of these tasks*	

Signed (Employee): *Chris Jonas*　　　　**Date:** *03/05/00*

Signed (Employment Officer): *Steve Leach*　　　　**Date:** *03/05/00*　　　　**Review Date:** *04/08/00*

Development Plan Part Three

Client Name:: *Chris Jonas*

This is the result of the information from the Ongoing Support Review Process (3–6 months into employment) including the vocational profile, job analysis and any employer appraisal review available. This helps both the employee and employer identify areas for development. This may include proposing further changes in the job itself, work environment, support mechanisms or the employee themselves. Future areas of development should be documented in the table below.

Summary of the Ongoing Support Review for the client

The review considered any movement in the VP and JA and whether the action plan from the DP part 2 have been met. The job has remained substantially the same and this has worked well for Chris, who likes the regularity of the work. The changes made to the 2 tasks have been partially successful with Chris now able to work with the support available on one task but still having difficulty with the other (tree pruning) as he needs regular encouragement. The HG is pleasantly surprised at how well Chris is working and enjoys his enthusiasm and conscientiousness.

Objectives	By Whom	Start Date	Finish Date	Performance Indicator (How will the objective be completed?)	Comments
Job supporter to focus on the tree pruning with Chris	*Job supporter*	*Now*	*01/12/00*	*Chris able to work for two hours without the need for instruction*	
Give Chris a rota for mornings and afternoons	*HG*	*12/09/00*	*01/12/00*	*Chris able to work through a morning or afternoon with minimum supervision on at least 3 days of 5*	*HG will monitor this for the period*
Chris to visit the local horticultural college and discuss a basic course	*Chris and job developer*	*Now*	*30/09/00*	*Meeting attended by Chris to see college tutor*	*If appropriate then fix up a start date*

Signed (Employee): *Chris Jonas*

Signed (Employment Officer): *Steve Leach*

Date: *04/08/00*

Date: *04/08/00*   **Review Date:** *01/12/00*

Development Plan Part Four

Client Name: *Chris Jonas*

Full review of the supported employment process: vocational profile and job analysis review, Support Review Charts and any other relevant information (6–12 months from start of employment). This should include a plan for progression to unsupported employment. If not then undertake another Ongoing Support Review to aid further developments.

Summary of the Overall Job Review (OJR) for the client (use information from all previous reviews)

The review saw a marked improvement in the way in which Chris was able to work with minimum support and he is now able to undertake all the tasks independently with only the minimum supervision from the HG. There have been a couple of problems when things happened unexpectedly and caused Chris some confusion as he found it difficult to adjust. He is undertaking an NVQ level 1 in horticulture and is doing well. Whilst we haven't yet got to looking at unsupported employment, both Chris and the HG can envisage a time when this could be a possibility.

Objectives	By Whom	Start Date	Finish Date	Performance Indicator (How will the objective be completed?)	Comments
HG to work with Chris on some 'crisis management' – if this happened what should you do?	HG and Chris	Now	01/07/01	Chris able to be given a scenario in which something unusual happens and he can offer ideas to sort it out or call for assistance	
Chris to complete the NVQ	Chris	Ongoing	30/05/01	Certificate achieved	
Consider the timescale for a withdrawal of support	HG	Now	01/07/01	Date set for Chris to move to unsupported employment	

Signed (Employee): *Chris Jonas*   **Date:** *01/12/00*

Signed (Employment Officer): *Steve Leach*   **Date:** *01/12/00*   **Review Date:** *01/07/01*

Appendix 5

Job-finding Form   Name:

Organisation:						
Address:						
Town:			Postcode:			
Telephone:			Email:			
Contact name:			Position:			
Nature of business						
Contact type	SEP	DEA	Employee	Cold call	Advert	Other
Contact details (potential issues, concerns, discussion points):						
Initial meeting	Date		Employee present?: yes/no			
Discussion issues						
Job analysis discussed?:		yes/no				
Progression discussed?:		yes/no				
Agreement discussed?:		yes/no				
Start date discussed?:		yes/no	Date:			
Other issues/action points/barriers to employment identified?						
Employee visit arranged?:		yes/no		Date:		
Visit (issues raised)						
Support needs discussed?:		yes/no				
Development plan discussed?:		yes/no				
Start date agreed?:		yes/no	Date:			

Appendix 6a

<table>
<tr><td colspan="2">

Job Analysis Form

</td></tr>
<tr><td colspan="2">

Although it is common practice to set out the basic aspects of a job for new recruits, it is not common for all aspects of the job and environment to be examined. People with disabilities are, in general, less familiar with working environments and a lot that would be taken for granted by an able-bodied person could actually be an area where the person with a disability needs some assistance or alteration to working practice.

The main aims of conducting the JA are to provide information regarding different aspects of the job to help with job matching and to identify aspects of the job where the person is likely to require specialist assistance.

This should be positive for both employee and employer; the employee will be able to highlight any 'gaps' in the working environment that need resolving at the start, and the employer is able to get a clear picture of the skill match between the new employee and the job. It is, therefore, vital that we gather all the details pertaining to the employer and the job. Please complete the details below as fully as possible and note any issues for discussion at the first meeting.

</td></tr>
<tr><td colspan="2">

1. Company Details

</td></tr>
<tr><td colspan="2">Organisation:</td></tr>
<tr><td colspan="2">Address:</td></tr>
<tr><td colspan="2"></td></tr>
<tr><td>Town:</td><td></td></tr>
<tr><td>Telephone:</td><td>Email:</td></tr>
<tr><td>Contact name:</td><td>Position:</td></tr>
<tr><td colspan="2">Business:</td></tr>
<tr><td>Supervisor:</td><td>Title:</td></tr>
<tr><td>Natural Support:</td><td>Title:</td></tr>
<tr><td>Number of employees on worksite</td><td>company total (if different):</td></tr>
<tr><td colspan="2">

2. Job Details

</td></tr>
<tr><td colspan="2">Job title:</td></tr>
<tr><td colspan="2">Job description available: yes/no (include brief details: the full details can be noted in the 'Job tasks' section on the next page)</td></tr>
<tr><td colspan="2">

</td></tr>
</table>

Work hours	Mon	Tues	Wed	Thurs	Fri	Sat	Sun
Start:							
Finish:							
Paid Hours:							

Total Paid Hours:						
Rate of pay:		Pay scale:		Pay review date:		
Overtime	Y/N	Bonus	Y/N	Increment	Y/N	PRP	Y/N

Details:

Timekeeping policy	Yes/no	Details	
Dress code	Yes/no	Details	
In-house training	Yes/no	Details	
Company pension	Yes/no	Details	
Notice period	Yes/no	Details	
Family relationship	Yes/no	Details	
Union	Yes/no	Details	
Sick pay	Yes/no	Details	
Holidays	Yes/no	Details	
Company appraisal	Yes/no	Details	

Health and safety (use the Risk Assessment list and H & S assessment forms)

Written policy	Yes/no	Details	
Risk assessment	Yes/no	Details	
H and S assessment done	Yes/no	Details	

Job development prospects (consider all training/promotion/job change potential)

Job flexibility (e.g. teamwork, independent working, hours, environment)

Job tasks
i. Tasks that occur every workday, identified by employer (core work routines)
ii. Tasks that occur on an irregular basis, identified by employer (episodic work routines)
iii. Tasks that underpin the job, e.g. use of protective clothing, proper use of breaks (**job-related routines**)
Other information (i.e. workplace culture issues–important rules, often unwritten)
Equipment and materials used: is it all supplied? yes/no
Amount of independence required
Level of supervision available
No. of co-workers in regular contact
Any other considerations (e.g. speed, quality, communication, special skills, etc.)

Physical ability (requirements of the job, not individual's abilities)

Standing	Yes/No	Details	
Walking	Yes/No	Details	
Sitting	Yes/No	Details	
Lifting	Yes/No	Details	
Carrying	Yes/No	Details	
Pushing	Yes/No	Details	
Climbing	Yes/No	Details	
Balancing	Yes/No	Details	
Bending	Yes/No	Details	
Kneeling	Yes/No	Details	
Manual handling	one hand	Yes/No	both hands	Yes/No
Manual dexterity	fine-motor	Yes/No	gross motor	Yes/No
Visual	Yes/No	Details	
Perceptual	Yes/No	Details	
Hearing	Yes/No	Details	
Other	Yes/No	Details	

Accommodations required (changes to regular routines, based on information from the VP and JSA. Identify potential resolution, timescales, outside expertise to be considered.)

Supervisor/natural support expectations (an interview with direct supervisor/support would be useful here as they may identify other considerations or concerns)

Signature of supervisor/support: Date:

N.B.: Issues raised here could become part of the training and development plan.

Employer Job Characteristics/Requirements (matches up to the vocational profile grid)

This grid identifies the closeness of the match by checking key environmental and job-specific characteristics. A mark in box 1 indicates the job characteristic is reflected in the statement on the left of the scale, a mark in box 9 indicates the job characteristic is reflected in the statement on the right of the scale, and a mark in box 5 indicates no preference.

Add any job characteristics to the list that you feel are relevant. Add any narrative on the grid or using a continuation sheet that will offer clarity and help with the job-matching process.

The intention is to match your job needs to the client's profile to identify potential job matches.

The job is:	1	2	3	4	5	6	7	8	9	
full time										part time (<16 hours)
indoors										outdoors
staying in one place										moving about
in a busy workplace										in a relaxed workplace
in a hot workplace										in a cold workplace
in a noisy workplace										in a quiet workplace
in a clean workplace										in a messy workplace
constantly – one job										doing different tasks
in a big workplace										in a small workplace
mainly with men										mainly with women
in a uniform										without a uniform
with words/books										not with words
with numbers										not with numbers
using public transport										not using public transport
with others										not with others

Please add any other job characteristics that you feel are relevant:

Skills needed	1	2	3	4	5	6	7	8	9	
use hands										Not needed
good eyesight										Not needed
good hearing										Not needed
communicate well										Not needed
lift heavy loads										Not needed
has stamina										Not needed
can read										Not needed
can use numbers										Not needed
can use money										Not needed
can tell time										Not needed
can work quickly										Not needed
can achieve quality										Not needed
can concentrate >2hrs										Not needed
can do varied tasks										One or two tasks only
has good balance										Not needed
can walk										Not needed
can stand for >2hrs										Not needed
can sit for >2hrs										Not needed
can use stairs										Not needed
doesn't often get angry										Not needed
can remember instructions										Not needed
can use the phone										Not needed
can drive										Not needed
can use a computer										Not needed
can spell										Not needed
has good handwriting										Not needed
can use judgement										Not needed
can work without support										Direct support needed
can use initiative										Not needed
can look after appearance										Not needed
has good personal hygiene										Not needed
Add any other skills that you feel are important to you										

Support needs checklist		Enter code below
Write in last column which code number most accurately reflects the employee's support needs		1 = need full support
		2 = need some support
General	Evidence/information/examples	3 = no support needed
Timekeeping		
Attendance		
Communication		
Behaviour		
Dress / appearance		
Social interaction		
Work-related skills		
Motivation		
Flexibility		
Initiative		
Team-skills		
H&S		
Consistency		
Working under pressure		

Work tasks (identified in job description, if applicable, i.e only when a particular job is identified or the client is already in employment)

a)		
b)		
c)		
d)		
e)		
f)		
g)		
h)		
i)		
j)		
k)		
l)		

Comments

Review date agreed:

Information Analysis/Review

This is where all the information is gathered together during the JA process and a review of the accommodations, adaptations, flexibilities needed based on that information and discussion with the employer. This is the ground work for the action points to be agreed which will be written in the Development Plan derived from the job-matching meeting. Both employment officer and employer should initial this review.

Initials: Employer: Employment Officer:

Appendix 6b

Job Analysis Form

Although it is common practice to set out the basic aspects of a job for new recruits, it is not common for all aspects of the job and environment to be examined. People with disabilities are, in general, less familiar with working environments and a lot that would be taken for granted by an able-bodied person could actually be an area where the person with a disability needs some assistance or alteration to working practice.

The main aims of conducting the JA are to provide information regarding different aspects of the job to help with job matching and to identify aspects of the job where the person is likely to require specialist assistance.

This should be positive for both employee and employer; the employee will be able to highlight any 'gaps' in the working environment that need resolving at the start, and the employer is able to get a clear picture of the skill match between the new employee and the job. It is, therefore, vital that we gather all the details pertaining to the employer and the job. Please complete the details below as fully as possible and note any issues for discussion at the first meeting.

1. Company Details

Organisation: *Pall Mall Renovations*

Address: *The Strand*

Town: *London*	
Telephone:	Email:
Contact name: *H.M. Jesty*	Position: *Production Director*

Business: Royal Upholsterers

Supervisor: *H.R. Prince*	Title: *Team Leader*
Natural Support: *P. Equerry*	Title: *Production worker*
Number of employees on worksite: *23*	company Total (if different):

2. Job Details

Job title: *Royal Renovations Operative*

Job description available: yes/no (include brief details: the full details can be noted in the 'Job tasks' section on the next page)

Repairing and renovating returned furniture
Making fabric swatches for customers

Work hours	Mon	Tues	Wed	Thurs	Fri	Sat	Sun
Start:	7.30	7.30	7.30	7.30	7.30		
Finish:	16.15	16.15	16.15	16.15	13.15		
Paid Hours:							

Total Paid Hours:	39						

Rate of pay: £5.35ph		Pay scale: Prod.op.		Pay review date:			01/02/02
Overtime	Y/N̶	Bonus	Y̶/N	Increment	Y̶/N	PRP	Y̶/N

Details:
Overtime is available but not compulsory and paid at time and half.

Timekeeping policy	Yes/n̶o̶	Details	Formal, timeclock, see company regs
Dress code	Yes/n̶o̶	Details	Casual, safety clothing when necessary
In-house training	Yes/n̶o̶	Details	Personal training record, NVQ for all
Company pension	Yes/n̶o̶	Details	Money purchase scheme, 3% employee/employer
Notice period	Yes/n̶o̶	Details	Weekly statutory
Family relationship	Y̶e̶s̶/no	Details	
Union	Y̶e̶s̶/no	Details	Individual union membership OK
Sick pay	Yes/n̶o̶	Details	£50p.w. on top of SSP for 4 weeks
Holidays	Yes/n̶o̶	Details	22 days p.a. + 8 statutory days
Company appraisal	Y̶e̶s̶/no	Details	

Health and Safety (use the Risk Assessment list and H&S assessment forms)

Written policy	Yes/n̶o̶	Details	Copy in each dept. + employee file
Risk assessment	Yes/n̶o̶	Details	Every job, update annually
H and S assessment done	Y̶e̶s̶/no	Details	Company H&S file seen - adequate

Job development prospects (concider all training/promotion/job change potential)

The person can move on as the job has an inspection remit. Post of product examiner would be the natural next step if things worked out.

Job flexibility (e.g. teamwork, independent working, hours, environment)

Small team but working on own tasks, hours can be flexible. Sometimes there is a need to work on job together so the team must work co-operatively and get on well.

i. Tasks that occur every workday, identified by employer (core work routines)
Removal of material from furniture to be repaired
Repair of furniture inc. refitting wooden parts, filling in, sanding, staining and varnishing.
Preparation of new materials – cutting to pattern, stitching, tacking, stapling
Tidying and preparing work area

ii. Tasks that occur on an irregular basis, identified by employer (episodic work routines)
Receipt of goods into dept./removal of goods out
Ordering of materials

iii. Tasks that underpin the job, e.g. use of protective clothing, proper use of breaks (job-related routines)
Use of chemicals
Use of safety clothing
Liaison with production dept.

Other information (i.e. workplace culture issues–important rules, often unwritten)
Relaxed workplace with teamwork an important aspect
Careful use of expensive materials very important
Customer confidentiality vital

Equipment and materials used: is it all supplied? yes/no
Stapling machines, sanders, hydraulic tables, sewing machinery, material cutters
Cleaning chemicals, varnish, staining liquids
Cloth material covering
Wooden parts
Safety goggles, eye glasses, face masks and overalls
Safety shoes – one pair per annum

Amount of independence required
Job is 80% self-managing given the variety of repairs and renovations.
Need to prioritise tasks and ensure enough materials available to complete jobs

Level of supervision available
High – supervisor works in same dept. and is available continuously during working hours

No. of co-workers in regular contact
3 in same area, 4 others in same dept.

Any other considerations (e.g. speed, quality, communication, special skills, etc.)
The need for quality and careful work is high given the expense of the materials used. Even if an order is needed quickly the need to maintain a high quality is an imperative.

Physical ability (requirements of the job, not individuals abilities)

Standing	Yes/~~No~~	Details	*Bench work, cutting, repairing etc.*	
Walking	Yes/~~No~~	Details	*Moving around work area, collecting materials*	
Sitting	Yes/~~No~~	Details	*sewing*	
Lifting	Yes/~~No~~	Details	*Small items alone, help with large pieces*	
Carrying	Yes/~~No~~	Details	*Materials and parts*	
Pushing	~~Yes~~/No	Details		
Pulling	~~Yes~~/No	Details		
Climbing	~~Yes~~/No	Details		
Balancing	~~Yes~~/No	Details		
Bending	Yes/~~No~~	Details	*Over work bench, removing old material*	
Kneeling	~~Yes~~/No	Details		
Manual handling	One hand	Yes/No	both hands	Yes/~~No~~
Manual dexterity	fine-motor	Yes/~~No~~	gross motor	Yes/~~No~~
Visual	Yes/~~No~~	Details	*Ensuring repairs are accurate*	
Perceptual	Yes/~~No~~	Details	*Judging material needed*	
Hearing	~~Yes~~/No	Details		
Other	~~Yes~~/No	Details		

Accommodations required (changes to regular routines, based on information from the VP and JSA. Identify potential resolution, timescales, outside expertise to be considered.)

Use of automatic stapler needed – weakness in left hand
Hydraulic table – help with lifting furniture

Supervisor/natural support expectations (an interview with direct supervisor/support would be useful here as they may identify other considerations or concerns)

Need for someone to work closely with other repairers to improve efficiency
Need for someone also able to work on tasks under own steam
Need for high quality output – someone who is careful and consistent.

Signature of supervisor/support: Date:

N.B.: Issues raised here could become part of the training and development plan.

Employer Job Characteristics/Requirements (matches up to the vocational profile grid)

This grid identifies the closeness of the match by checking key environmental and job-specific characteristics. A mark in box 1 indicates the job characteristic is reflected in the statement on the left of the scale, a mark in box 9 indicates the job characteristic is reflected in the statement on the right of the scale, and a mark in box 5 indicates no preference.

Add any job characteristics to the list that you feel are relevant. Add any narrative on the grid or using a continuation sheet that will offer clarity and help with the job-matching process.

The intention is to match your job needs to the client's profile to identify potential job matches.

The job is…	1	2	3	4	5	6	7	8	9	
full time	x									part time (<16 hours)
indoors	x									outdoors
staying in one place						x				moving about
in a busy workplace			x							in a relaxed workplace
in a hot workplace				x						in a cold workplace
in a noisy workplace			x							in a quiet workplace
in a clean workplace			x							in a messy workplace
Constantly – one job							x			doing different tasks
in a big workplace				x						in a small workplace
mainly with men			x							mainly with women
in a uniform							x			without a uniform
with words/books							x			not with words
with numbers							x			not with numbers
using public transport		x								not using public transport
with others	x									not with others

Please add any other job characteristics that you feel are relevant:

Skills needed	1	2	3	4	5	6	7	8	9	
use hands		x								Not needed
good eyesight		x								Not needed
good hearing				x						Not needed
communicate well			x							Not needed
lift heavy loads				x						Not needed
have stamina				x						Not needed
can read					x					Not needed
can use numbers					x					Not needed
can use money									x	Not needed
can tell time		x								Not needed
can work quickly							x			Not needed
can achieve quality	x									Not needed
can concentrate >2hrs			x							Not needed
can do varied tasks		x								One or two tasks only
have good balance					x					Not needed
can walk			x							Not needed
can stand for >2hrs		x								Not needed
can sit for >2hrs		x								Not needed
can use stairs								x		Not needed
doesn't often get angry								x		Not needed
can remember instructions			x							Not needed
can use the phone									x	Not needed
can drive									x	Not needed
can use a computer									x	Not needed
can spell									x	Not needed
have good handwriting									x	Not needed
can use judgement		x								Not needed
can work without support		x								Direct support needed
can use initiative		x								Not needed
can look after appearance					x					Not needed
have good personal hygiene			x							Not needed

Add any other skills that you feel are important to you

Support needs checklist Write in last column which code number most accurately reflects the employee's support needs		Enter code below 1 = need Full support 2 = need some support
General	**Evidence/information/examples**	3 = no support needed
Timekeeping	*Never late*	*3*
Attendance	*Exemplary*	*3*
Communication	*Always asks for help*	*3*
Behaviour	*Respects all staff, helps co-workers with work*	*3*
Dress / appearance	*Clean and tidy*	*3*
Social Interaction	*A little reluctant, will listen to others without offering to add anything*	*2*
Work-related skills		
Motivation	*Can need help when changing tasks*	*2*
Flexibility	*Willing to do but needs support*	*2*
Initiative	*Good within task, can solve minor problems*	*2*
Team-skills	*Very sensitive to others and helps in all ways*	*3*
H&S	*Very careful and always wears safety equipment*	*3*
Consistency	*Same quality of work at end of day as at start*	*3*
Working under pressure	*Needs some reassurance*	*2*

Work tasks (identified in job description, if applicable, i.e only when a particular job is identified or the client is already in employment)

a)	*Removal of material from furniture*	
b)	*Refitting wooden parts*	
c)	*Filling in–using wood filler, polyfiller*	
d)	*Sanding*	
e)	*Staining*	
f)	*Varnishing*	
g)	*Cutting to pattern*	
h)	*Stitching*	
i)	*Tacking, stapling*	
j)	*Tidying and preparing work area*	

Comments

Review date agreed:

Information Analysis/Review

This is where all the information is gathered together during the JA process and a review of the accommodations, adaptations, flexibilities needed based on that information and discussion with the employer. This is the ground work for the action points to be agreed which will be written in the Development Plan derived from the job-matching meeting. Both employment officer and employer should initial this review.

Leslie has worked at Pall Mall for 5 years as a machinist. She had a stroke, right-side hemiplegia, now has an eye problem and standing is becoming increasingly difficult. Recent redundancies and employer looking at re-deployment.

Repairs and renovations being considered (Leslie has worked there previously) but will need some support, at least initially, to undertake the new duties. Aids and adaptations are being considered, in particular a hydraulic table, and specialist tools to support her weaker right side.

Whilst there is some sewing included it is not piece rate. Making up new swatches being considered and a possibility of a role as an examiner could be available in the future.

Leslie has the ability to work unsupervised but will need some support to get to that position. This should help develop her self-confidence by ensuring that the jobs undertaken are fully explained and ones in which she can succeed with the necessary training.

Leslie is going to need support when changing tasks so that she has the confidence and knowledge to move onto new tasks by herself.

This will need a full outline in the development plan and should be reviewed within 6 weeks to offer her time to settle in but not too long without support if things are not working out in some areas.

Initials: Employer: Employment Officer:

Appendix 7a

Health and Safety Checklist

Common things to look for when setting up a new job or during review

Housekeeping

- Are work areas clean and tidy?
- Is dirt and refuse removed at least daily from floors and work stations?

Overcrowding

- Is there risk of injury from overcrowding or poor workplace layout?

Temperature

- Is the temperature reasonable for the work undertaken?

Lighting

- Is the lighting sufficient and suitable for the work undertaken?

Sanitary Accommodation

- Are there sufficient and suitable sanitary conveniences?

Guarding of Dangerous Machinery

- Are all dangerous or moving parts of machinery securely guarded?

Other Dangerous Equipment

- Are there any problems with or hazards arising from cranes, lifts, hoists, forklift trucks, electrical equipment?
- Are air lines and receivers regularly inspected to ensure they are safe?

Noise

- Are there problems with noise?

Safety of floors, stairs etc.

Are all floors, passages, walkways, steps and stairs

- of a sound construction?
- well maintained?
- free from obstruction?
- free from liquids, oil and slippery substances?

Fire

- Have alarms been tested in the last three months?
- Are all fire exits properly maintained and free from obstruction?
- Are all flammable materials and liquids properly stored?

Welfare

Are there suitable

- washing facilities?
- seating facilities?
- places for storing/drying clothes?
- canteen/rest room facilities away from the workplace?

First Aid

- Are there adequate First Aid facilities?
- Are the location of First Aid facilities and First Aiders clearly displayed?

Substances Hazardous to Health

- Are workers protected against exposure to dust, fumes and substances hazardous to health?

Eye Protection

- Are there suitable goggles or screens provided for eye protection in dangerous processes?
- Are eye tests provided and glasses supplied free of charge to regular DSE users?

Lifting

- Are workers expected to lift, carry or move loads or objects that are likely to cause injury?

Training

- Do all workers receive training in their jobs, especially where machinery is involved?
- Are all young persons, or those considered more at risk, properly supervised?

Recording of Incidents

- Are all accidents, dangerous occurrences, incidents, near misses and occupational diseases specified and recorded?
- Is a suitable accident book available?

Information

Is there adequate information provided

- under Section 2(2)(c) of HASAWA and the Safety Representatives and Safety Committees Regulations?
- by HSE or Local Authority Inspectors under Section 28(1) of HASAWA?

Appendix 7b

Health and Safety Assessment Checklist

Page 1 of this Health and Safety Checklist should be completed when the employee is being initially assessed for suitability. The remaining pages should be completed on the first monitoring visit thereafter, and used, if required, for subsequent monitoring and review.

Date of visit	
Employer	
Address	
Contact	
H and S contact	
Tel no	
Fax no	
Job developer	

Insurance	Expires	Displayed	Seen
Employers liability			
Public liability			

Comments:

Registration	
Registered with Health and Safety Executive?	Yes/No
Registered with Local Authority?	Yes/No

Comments:

Health and Safety Policy	
Health and Safety policy seen?	Yes/No
Are employees made aware of the policy and revisions when they occur?	Yes/No

Comments:

Risk Assessments Have all or any of the following been carried out?:	Date
General risk assessment	
Display screen equipment	
Manual handling	
COSHH	
Noise	

Comments:

Training and Supervision	
Will client be adequately supervised?	Yes/No
Will appropriate induction training, including health and safety be given?	Yes/No
Comments:	

Fire and Emergency Procedures	
Is training given in evacuation procedures, including outside work ?	Yes/No
Are regular fire drills carried out?	Yes/No
Are fire extinguishers appropriate and regularly serviced?	Yes/No
Are fire doors/exits free of obstruction and clearly marked?	Yes/No
Is a notice giving location of fire exits and assembly points displayed?	Yes/No
Is a Fire Certificate held?	Yes/No
If NO, has a Certificate been applied for?	Yes/No
Are appropriate precautions taken to minimise hazards?	Yes/No
Are health and safety hazard warning signs displayed?	Yes/No
Comments:	

First Aid and Accident Reporting Systems	
Is there an 'Accident Book'?	Yes/No
Does employer record all accidents?	Yes/No
Does employer record 'near miss' incidents?	Yes/No
Does employer understand requirements of RIDDOR?	Yes/No
Are there trained First Aiders?	Yes/No
If NO, are there competent persons?	Yes/No
Are First Aid boxes provided?	Yes/No
Are names and locations of trained First Aiders/Competent Persons displayed?	Yes/No
Comments:	

Working Conditions

Comments:

Machinery, Equipment and Systems

Comments:

Hazardous Substances/Materials

Comments:

General

Comments:

Any Special Features of the Placement

Bearing in mind the client's disability are there any specific hazards which may relate to the placement?

Comments

Appendix 8a

Job Matching Form   Name:

VP completed	Date:	JA completed	Date:

Organisation:

Job:

Accomodations/Gaps Identified

Compare Employee Skills/Preferences Grid (VP) with Employer Job Characteristics/Requirements Grid (JA)

Job-Matching Issues (Note all issues and potential resolution)

Is the match acceptable to client and employer?	yes/no

Reasons:

Confirm the action now to be undertaken	
Negotiate employment with present employer	[ ]
Job Search renewed	[ ]
Referral to other appropriate service	[ ]
Referral back to DEA	[ ]
Other (note down any reasons or information)	[ ]

Signed:	Date:

Appendix 8b

Job Matching Form

Name:

VP completed	Date: *21/04/98*	JA completed	Date: *04/06/98*

Organisation: *Apple Pie Bedcovers Ltd*

Job: *machinist*

Accomodation/Gaps Identified

- *Rachel needs extra time to understand new tasks and a calm job supporter.*
- *In complex job tasks it would be preferable to break the job down into its simple components for training purposes.*
- *One job at a time rather than a list of jobs to be completed.*
- *Support will be needed to help Rachel develop her initiative on new jobs – when things go wrong or something unusual happens. This could mean that Rachel will need training in how things go wrong and how to put it right as well as regular job task training.*

Compare Employee Skills/Preferences Grid (VP) with Employer Job Characteristics/Requirements Grid (JA)

Close match in most areas, or if not they are not significant areas.
Rachel wants a full-time job but only 32 hours on offer.
Busy work environment may cause Rachel some difficulties.
The need to remember instructions is a major gap.
Being able to achieve consistent quality also an issue.

Job-Matching Issues (Note all issues and potential resolution)

Instructions – employer willing to look at listing instructions for Rachel to keep with her.
Hours – Rachel will work for the 32 hours for 6 months and employer will review in light of job review.
Quality – Rachel will work closely with one co-worker who has trained many staff in the tasks and this will be reviewed in 6 months.

Is the match acceptable to client and employer?	yes/~~no~~

Reasons:

Employer impressed with Rachel's enthusiasm and conscientiousness during the job taster.
Rachel liked the department and got on well with the supervisor and co-workers and it is close to her home.

Confirm the action now to be undertaken

Negotiate employment with present employer	[x]
Job Search renewed	[ ]
Referral to other appropriate service	[ ]
Referral back to DEA	[ ]
Other (note down any reasons or information)	[ ]

Signed: *Steve Leach*	Date: 01/01/01

Support Review – Client Chart

Client Name:

The Support Review Chart will help develop the relationship between the employee and employer by ensuring that progression in a range of job-related skills is formally noted and any weaknesses (on either side) are strengthened. Each party will make an assessment of performance within the four key categories: job task skills, communication skills, training and reliability. The scale is from 1 to 5, with 1 being 'never' and 5 being 'always'. Lower points (1,2) on the scale would indicate a less favourable position and higher points (4,5) a more favourable position. 3 would be average. The use of specific examples to support the assessment is vital and will help prevent participants giving arbitrary scores on review.

Review Date:	Never (1) – Always (5) Tick one box at each review		Progress	Examples to illustrate attainment level:
Job Tasks:	1 2 3 4 5	1 2 3 4 5		
A current job task list and/or job description should be attached to this chart. Consider: meets required work standard, able to perform different tasks, undertakes tasks independently, able to use own initiative.				
Communication:	1 2 3 4 5	1 2 3 4 5		
Consider: works well with others, builds social relationships, behaves appropriately, shows respect for others				
Training:	1 2 3 4 5	1 2 3 4 5		
Consider: willingness to keep to internal/external training, positively benefits from training experience.				
Reliability:	1 2 3 4 5	1 2 3 4 5		
Consider: time-keeping, punctuality, trusted with company resources.				
Overall Development Score				Overall Comments:
% of possible total				
Other/personal development e.g.	1 2 3 4 5			Client Signature: Date:
Consider: dressing appropriately for work, education, outside interests, achievements.				

Support Review – Employer Chart

Client Name:

Total scores within each category are added together to form an overall development score. Eventually, after the first review, progress can be compared with past scores to gauge how well the developing strategy is progressing. Ensure that a job list is attached to each Support Review Chart and any changes are identified during the next review process. The potential for development by trying out other job tasks could also be discussed with the client. When completing the Support Review Chart during a review visit, examples of each criterion are listed on the form to help you, the client and employer consider appropriate examples that illustrate the particular viewpoint.

Review Date:	Never (1) – Always (5) Tick one box at each review	Progress	Examples to illustrate attainment level:
Job Tasks: A current job task list and/or job description should be attached to this charts, Consider: meets required work standard, able to perform different tasks, undertakes tasks independently, able to use own initiative.	1 2 3 4 5 1 2 3 4 5		
Communication: Consider: works well with others, builds social relationships, behaves appropriately, shows respect for others	1 2 3 4 5 1 2 3 4 5		
Training: Consider: willingness to keep to internal/external training, positively benefits from training experience.	1 2 3 4 5 1 2 3 4 5		
Reliability: Consider: time-keeping, punctuality, trusted with company resources.	1 2 3 4 5 1 2 3 4 5		
Overall Development Score			**Overall Comments:**
% of possible total			
Other/personal development e.g. Consider: dressing appropriately for work, education, outside interests, achievements.	1 2 3 4 5		**Employer Signature:** Date:

Support Review – Client/Employer Chart   Client Name:

To reiterate, the Support Review Chart is based upon an evaluation of the client's progress in job-related skill areas. It is initially a quantitive evaluation but using qualitative examples to support the evaluation. Its purpose is to strengthen the relationship between the employer and employee by bringing them together to agree what progress is being made and what needs to be done in the future to sustain that development. It may identify a need for change in either the employer or employee and should be used primarily as a development tool not as a way to apportion blame for either lack of progress or lack of support.

Review Date:	Never (1) – Always (5) Tick one box at each review	Progress	Meeting date: Comments at joint meeting
Job Tasks Employee	1 2 3 4 5 1 2 3 4 5		
Employer	1 2 3 4 5 1 2 3 4 5		
A current job task list and/or job description should be attached to this chart, Concider: meets required work standard, able to perform different tasks, undertakes tasks independently, able to use own initiative.			
Communication: Employee	1 2 3 4 5 1 2 3 4 5		
Employer	1 2 3 4 5 1 2 3 4 5		
Consider: works well with others, builds social relationships, behaves appropriately, shows respect for others			
Training: Employee			
Employer	1 2 3 4 5 1 2 3 4 5		
Consider: willingness to keep to internal/external training, positively benefits from training experience.			
Reliability: Employee			
Employer	1 2 3 4 5 1 2 3 4 5		
Consider: time-keeping, punctuality, trusted with company resources.			
Client Overall Development Score			Overall Comments:
Employer Overall Development Score			
Client % of possible total			Client Signature:
Employer % of possible total			Employer Signature:
Other/personal development e.g.	1 2 3 4 5 1 2 3 4 5		Date:
Consider: dressing appropriately for work, education, outside interests, achievements.			

Support Review – Client Chart

Client Name: *Christine*

The Support Review Chart will help develop the relationship between the employee and employer by ensuring that progression in a range of job-related skills is formally noted and any weaknesses (on either side) are strengthened. Each party will make an assessment of performance within the four key categories: job task skills, communication skills, training and reliability. The scale is from 1 to 5, with 1 being 'never' and 5 being 'always'. Lower points (1,2) on the scale would indicate a less favourable position and higher points (4,5) a more favourable position. 3 would be average. The use of specific examples to support the assessment is vital and will help prevent participants giving arbitrary scores on review.

Review Date:	Never (1) – Always (5) Tick one box at each review		Progress	Examples to illustrate attainment level:
	30/08/99	30/08/00		
Job Tasks:	1 2 3 ✓4 5	1 2 3 4 ✓5	1	*Now using the machinery in the new factory, has helped to fix small problems with the machinery e.g. the tracking belt keeps slipping off and I can fix it.*
A current job task list and/or job description should be attached to this chart. Consider: meets required work standard, able to perform different tasks, undertakes tasks independently, able to use own initiative.				
Communication:	1 2 3 4 ✓5	1 2 3 4 ✓5	0	*Poor start to the year with a problem with a co-worker was resolved and things have improved a lot.*
Consider: works well with others, builds social relationships, behaves appropriately, shows respect for others				*I am working well in a team.*
Training:	1 2 3 4 ✓5	1 2 3 4 ✓5	0	*I have set jobs which I like doing, but can train on new ones if needed.*
Consider: willingness to keep to internal/external training, positively benefits from training experience.				
Reliability:	1 2 3 4 ✓5	1 2 3 4 ✓5	0	*I am never late.*
Consider: time-keeping, punctuality, trusted with company resources.				*I always take my breaks on time.*
Overall Development Score	19	20	1	Overall Comments:
% of possible total	95	100	5%	*I am doing quite well in the new factory.*
Other/personal development e.g.	1 2 3 ✓4 5	1 2 3 ✓4 5	1	Client Signature:
Consider: dressing appropriately for work, education, outside interests, achievements.				Date:

Support Review – Employer Chart

Client Name: *Christine*

Total scores within each category are added together to form an overall development score. Eventually, after the first review, progress can be compared with past scores to gauge how well the developing strategy is progressing. Ensure that a job list is attached to each Support Review Chart and any changes are identified during the next review process. The potential for development by trying out other job tasks could also be discussed with the client. When completing the Support Review Chart during a review visit, examples of each criterion are listed on the form to help you, the client and employer consider appropriate examples that illustrate the particular viewpoint.

	Never (1) – Always (5) Tick one box at each review	Progress	Examples to illustrate attainment level:
Review Date:			
Job Tasks: A current job task list and/or job description should be attached to this chart. Consider: meets required work standard, able to perform different tasks, undertakes tasks independently, able to use own initiative.	1 2 ✓3 4 5 1 2 3 ✓4 5	1	Just gets on with allocated duties. Always needs supervision. If there is a problem she finds it difficult to sort it out.
Communication: Consider: works well with others, builds social relationships, behaves appropriately, shows respect for others	1 2 3 ✓4 5 1 2 ✓3 4 5	-1	She says very little to others in the team. She is quiet at break times, likes to listen rather than contribute. Does enjoy nights out.
Training: Consider: willingness to keep to internal/external training, positively benefits from training experience.	1 2 3 ✓4 5 1 2 3 ✓4 5	0	Has taken some new jobs on but prefers her regular work. She is happy to train at work but would find it very difficult to do external training; she doesn't like the college courses.
Reliability: Consider: time-keeping, punctuality, trusted with company resources.	1 2 3 4 ✓5 1 2 3 4 ✓5	0	Christine is the best time-keeper we have. She is very honest.
Overall Development Score	15 16	1	**Overall Comments:**
% of possible total	75 80	5%	Christine is a reliable employee but needs to show more initiative. Christine needs lots of supervision.
Other/personal development e.g. Consider: dressing appropriately for work, education, outside interests, achievements.	1 2 ✓3 4 5 1 2 ✓3 4 5	0	Employer Signature: Date:

Support Review – Client/Employer Chart

Client Name: *Christine*

To reiterate, the Support Review Chart is based upon an evaluation of the client's progress in job-related skill areas. It is initially a quantitive evaluation but using qualitative examples to support the evaluation. Its purpose is to strengthen the relationship between the employer and employee by bringing them together to agree what progress is being made and what needs to be done in the future to sustain that development. It may identify a need for change in either the employer or employee and should be used primarily as a development tool not as a way to apportion blame for either lack of progress or lack of support.

Review Date:	Never (1) – Always (5) Tick one box at each review		Progress	Meeting date: Comments at joint meeting:
Job Tasks				
Employee	1 2 3 ✓4 5	1 2 3 4 ✓5	1	*Employer had not realised that Christine could correct some of the problems she came*
Employer	1 2 ✓3 4 5	1 2 3 ✓4 5	1	*across. He had checked this with co-workers. However, there is a need to continue to develop her skills to include being able to become a self-starter.*

A current job task list and/or job description should be attached to this chart. Consider: meets required work standard, able to perform different tasks, undertakes tasks independently, able to use own initiative.

	Never (1) – Always (5)		Progress	Comments
Communication:				*Employer admits she doesn't need as much supervision as he first thought. Christine now realises that there is more to the job than she thought but she is willing to try to extend herself.*
Employee	1 2 3 4 ✓5	1 2 3 4 ✓5	0	*Employer realises that even though Christine is quiet she is not withdrawn and takes*
Employer	1 2 3 ✓4 5	1 2 ✓3 4 5	-1	*an interest in her co-workers exchanges. She will try and talk about things that interest her and build on that. She is seen as an important member of the group and never has a harsh word to say to anyone – a vital skill in any workforce.*

Consider: works well with others, builds social relationships, behaves appropriately, shows respect for others

	Never (1) – Always (5)		Progress	Comments
Training:				*Christine hasn't been more active in seeking training opportunities as she is concerned*
Employee	1 2 3 4 ✓5	1 2 3 4 ✓5	0	*that she will not understand and fail. She does want to learn new jobs but feels*
Employer	1 2 3 ✓4 5	1 2 3 ✓4 5	0	*she is incapable. Employer realises that he will have to approach training from a different angle and ensure that it is carefully structured to include Christine.*

Consider: willingness to keep to internal/external training, positively benefits from training experience.

	Never (1) – Always (5)		Progress	Comments
Reliability:				*Full agreement in this area and employer recognising that Christine is a vital member*
Employee	1 2 3 4 ✓5	1 2 3 4 ✓5	0	*of the workforce, completely reliable and this helps in planning work.*
Employer	1 2 3 4 ✓5	1 2 3 4 ✓5	0	

Consider: time-keeping, punctuality, trusted with company resources.

			Progress	Overall Comments:
Client Overall Development Score	19	20	1	*Employer has a clearer (and more positive) picture of Christine's contribution and will look more carefully at development issues.*
Employer Overall Development Score	15	16	1	*Christine has a more realistic idea about what is expected of her and feels happier about her contribution at work. She understands how to build on her current contribution.*
Client % of possible total	95	100	5	Client Signature:
Employer % of possible total	75	80	5	Employer signature: Date:

Consider: dressing appropriately for work, education, outside interests, achievements.

Appendix 10

Letter from job developer to client

Dear A,

Your employer has now recognised that you have a disability. Under the terms of the Disability Discrimination Act they need to show that adjustments have been made to take into account your dyspraxia. However, this does not mean that they must make more adjustments than they can reasonably support.

Despite some adjustments you should still be operating in line with the main features of an AA's duties. The 'technological or physical' items obtained for you to mitigate for your disability should now be in place. You should now be able to use them all as well as the other strategies we have been working on together.

It is a pity that long periods of sickness interfered with the smooth running of it all but I know your aim will be to get back to where you left off as soon as possible. I have suggested some actions to help this.

I was interested to hear about the work you are doing on Anger Management, and your counsellor's advice about containing your strong feelings about football. On reflection I realised that this may have a bearing in a way that I did not appreciate on Thursday. I feel that you may be unconsciously giving football a more important place in your life than you realise.

You will recall that I admired your haircut – and I do. However, when I looked back I realised that in conjunction with a (very smart and new) Celtic football shirt, the whole picture was that of a skinhead football fan. I really believe that you need to divorce yourself from football completely in the work situation. Consciously and unconsciously. You are dressed for the very situation in which you find anger and frustration hard to contain. When actors want to get into character they often start by wearing the character's clothes. It is a well known strategy – the clothes are a big part of the way they feel and react.

In fact I do not believe that it is an appropriate place for sporting gear at all. Casual – yes. Sports gear – no. For other reasons too I believe that it is unsuitable workwear.

- It suggests immaturity not maturity.

- It is not appropriate to your age.

- Sportswear – even expensive/designer sportswear is no longer fashionable but still worn on non-sporting occasions only by those who are either out-of-date or from a recognisable under-class. Study and analyse this whenever you can.

- Combined with a skinhead haircut it suggests aggression.

I believe that you should not be intimating any of these things in the workplace. I know that you still have hopes of future promotion. I would say that you will never be taken seriously until you give the appearance of seriousness. That does not mean a suit and tie but it does mean reflecting the inherent culture of the environment. Look at your colleagues and emulate the general dress-code of people of the grade above you. This includes footwear. This is standard advice for anyone interested in promotion. I enclose a photocopy of an article I read very recently which you may find helpful too.

I hope you will accept this in the spirit it is sent – as helpful and constructive. It is based on a long-term knowledge of the cultures of organisations – and the unfortunate realisation that appearances:

- give away more about us than we sometimes realise

- are the strongest means by which others make judgements about us

- indicate which social 'clan' we belong to

- indicate that we do not belong to the same 'clan' as those around us – which is fine so long as one is prepared to pay the price for it

- need to be appropriate

- show whether or not one can 'read' a situation and act accordingly.

I look forward to seeing you on the 28th,

Yours sincerely

Glossary

DEA	Disability Employment Adviser
DipSE	Diploma in Supported Employment
H&S	Health and Safety
JA	Job Analysis
JSA	Job Seekers Allowance
LSC	Learning and Skills Council (formerly the TEC)
OJR	Overall Job Review
OSR	Ongoing Support Review
PCP	Person Centred Planning
SE	Supported Employment
SEDI	Supported Employment Development Initiative
SEP	government funded Supported Employment Programme
SI	Systematic Instruction
SRC	Support Review Chart
TA	Task Analysis
TEC	Training and Enterprise Council (now LSC)
VP	Vocational Profile
Workstep	the new name for the supported employment programme

References

Bass, M. (2000) *Supported Employment for People with Learning Difficulties.* York: Joseph Rowntree Trust.www.jrf.org.uk/knowledge/findings/socialcare/sc86.htm

Beyer, S. , Jackson, T. and Everett, G. (1998) *Reforming the Supported Placement Scheme to Promote Career Development and Access for People with Greater Support Needs.* WCLDU / DfEE.

Bissonette, D. (1994) *Beyond Traditional Job Development.* California: Milt Wright and Associates Publishers.

Callahan, M. J. and Garner, J. B. (1997) *Keys to the Workplace.* Baltimore: Paul Brookes.

Cheshire County Council (1997) *Diploma in Supported Employment.* Cheshire: Cheshire County Council.

Frith, V. (ed) (1991) *Autism and Asperger Syndrome.* UK University Press.

Goode, S., Howlin, P. and Rutter, M. (1993) 'A cognitive and behavioural follow-up study of individuals with autism'. In P. Howlin (ed) *Autism, Preparing for Adulthood.* London: Routledge.

Hill, P. (2000) 'Is Employment Necessarily Therapeutic for People with Mental Health Problems?'. *A Life in the Day 4, 3,* (August). Brighton: Pavilion.

HSE (1999) Five Steps to Risk Assessment. Ref.INDG163 (rev1) Sheffield: HSE Books. Website: http://www.open.gov.uk/hsehome.htm

Johnstone, D. (1998) *An Introduction to Disability Studies.* London: David Fulton.

Kroese, B. S., Kahn, S. and Hearn, M. (1996) 'An Evaluation of Target Supported Employment Agency.' Rathbone Society Report, Birmingham 1996.

Mental Health Foundation (1999) 'Mental Health in the Workplace.' MHF report.

O'Bryan, A. *et al.* (2000) *A Framework for Supported Employment.* York: Joseph Rowntree Foundation.

Perkins, R., Buckfield, R. and Choy, D. (1997) 'Access to employment: a Supported Employment Project to enable mental health service users to obtain jobs within mental health teams.' *Journal of Mental Health 6,* 3, 307–318.

Pimm, P. (1997) *Challenging Behaviour and Cerebral Palsy.* London: Scope.

Priestley, M. (2000) 'Adults Only: Disability, Social Policy and the Life Course.' *Journal of Sociological Policy 29*, 3, 421–439.

Sutcliffe, J. (1991) *Education for Choice and Empowerment: Adults with Learning Difficulties.* Leicester: National Institute of Adult Continuing Education/OUP.

The Employment Service (1999) The Supported Employment Programme: A consultation on future development. ES Ref. No. SEPCD1.

The Employment Service (2001) *Workstep: a handbook for providers.*

ES Ref. No. DSSWHB.

Wehman, P., and Kregel, J. (1998) *More Than a Job.* Baltimore: Paul Brookes.

Yates, E. (1998) *Supported Employment: Towards a National View.* London: RNIB/DfEE.

Further Reading

Barnes, C. (1991) *Disabled People in Britain and Discrimination*. British Council of Disabled People.

Brisenden, S. (1986) 'Independent Living and the Medical Model of Disability.' *Disability, Handicap and Society 1*, 2, 173–178.

Curiel, F. (1997) *Take Charge of Your Job Search!: A Handbook to Empower Unemployed People to Find Their Own Jobs*. Florida: Training Resource Network Inc.

DiLeo, D., Luecking, R. and Hathaway, S. (1995) *Natural Supports in Action: Strategies to Facilitate Employer Supports of Workers with Disabilities*. Florida: Training Resource Network Inc.

DiLeo, D. and Langton, D. (eds) (1996) *Facing the Future: Best Practices in Supported Employment*. Florida: Training Resource Network Inc.

Drake, R. E., McHugo, D.R., Becker, D.R, Anthony, W.A. and Clark, R.E. (1996) 'The New Hampshire Study of Supported Employment for People with Severe Mental Illness.' *Journal of Consulting and Clinical Psychology 64*, 2, 391–399.

Hyde, M. (1998) 'Sheltered and Supported Employment in the 1990s: the experiences of disabled workers in the UK.' *Disability & Society 13*, 2, 199–215.

Kilsby, M. and Beyer, S. (1996) 'Engagement and Interaction: a comparison between supported employment and day service provision.' *Journal of Intellectual Disability Research 40*, 4, 348–357.

Mank, D. (1994) 'The Underachievement of Supported Employment: A Call for Reinvestment.' *Journal of Disability Policy Studies 5*, 2, 2–24.

Mank, D, Sandow, D. and Rhodes, L. (1991) 'Quality Assurance in Supported Employment: New Approaches to Improvement.' *Vocational Rehabilitation,* January, 59–68.

Martin, N., Johnston, G. and Stevens, P. (1999) 'Adults with Intellectual Disabilities and Challenging Behaviour in Supported Employment: Initial Findings.' *Journal of Applied Research in Intellectual Disabilities 12*, 2,149–156.

Murphy, S. T. and Rogan, P. (1994) *Developing Natural Supports in the Workplace: A Practitioner's Guide.* Florida: Training Resource Network Inc.

Neitupski, J., Verstegen, D. and Petty, D. M. (1995) *The Job Development Handbook: Facilitating Employer Decisions to Hire People with Disabilities.* Florida: Training Resource Network Inc.

Neitupski, J., Hamre-Neitupski, S. Vanderhart, N.S. and Fishback, K. (1996) 'Employer Perceptions of the Benefits and Concerns of Supported Employment.' *Education and Training in Mental Retardation and Developmental Disabilities,* December, 310–323.

Rhodes, L., Mank, D., Sandow, D. Buckley, J. and Albin, J. (1990) 'Supported Employment Implementation: Shifting from Program Monitoring to Quality Improvement.' *Journal of Disability Policy Studies 1,* 2, 2–18.

Shearn, J., Beyer, S. and Felce, D. (2000) 'The Cost-Effectiveness of Supported Employment for People with Severe Intellectual Disabilities and High Support Needs: A Pilot Study.' *Journal of Applied Research in Intellectual Disabilities 1,*13, 29–37.

Walker, C. (2000) 'User Views of Supported Employment.' Employment Service Research & Development Report ref. ESR40, May.

Walsh, P. N., Lynch, C. and deLacey, E. (1994) 'Supported Employment for Irish Adults with Intellectual Disability: The OPEN ROAD experience.' *International Journal of Rehabilitation Research 17,*15–24.

Wehman, P., West, M. and Kregel, J. (1999) 'Supported Employment Program Development and Research Needs: Looking Ahead to the Year 2000.' *Education and Training in Mental Retardation and Developmental Disabilities 34,* 1, 3–19.

Wehman, P., Krugel, J., Sherron, P., Nguyen, S., Kreutzer, J., Fry, R. and Zasler, N. (1993) 'Critical factors associated with the successful supported employment placement of patients with severe traumatic brain injury.' *Brain Injury 7,* 1, 31–44.

Subject index

Author index

CPSIA information can be obtained at www.ICGtesting.com
Printed in the USA
268682BV00002B/5/P